Problem Cats
and Their Owners

A Behavior and Training Handbook

Louis Vine, DVM

Cartoon Illustrations by Kate Salley Palmer

All photos by Isabelle Francais except the following: Joan Balzarini (pages 5, 6, 35, 66, 155), Richard K. Blackmon (pages 40, 54, 154), Aaron Davis (page 103), Jacquie DeLillo (pages 97, 109, 134), Michael G. Dempsey (page 68), Jacob Denham (pages 26, 27, 51, 152), Kim Gillenwater (page 69), Jeri Gloss (page 67), Gillian Lisle (pages 112, 141), C. Oakley (pages 43, 57, 135, 138, 145, 146), Robert Pearcy (pages 110, 118), Vince Serbin (pages 81, 91, 150), Linda Sturdy (pages 22, 30, 47, 59, 87, 124, 143, 147, 156), John Tyson (pages 15, 18, 89, 93, 100, 114, 153)

© T.F.H. Publications, Inc.

Table of Contents

Introduction

The popularity of cats is always increasing and, unfortunately, so is the number of cats with behavioral problems. It is no coincidence that the closer the cat's relationship to humans, the greater the increase in abnormal behavior. For instance, outdoor cats have fewer behavioral problems, but as the time spent indoors increases, so do the problems. When the owner interferes with the normal, natural needs of the pet, problems arise. Most cats are not born problem cats but become that

In all studies of cat behavior problems, the most important factor is the owner-pet relationship. A well-behaved cat probably has a healthy relationship with her owner.

way as a result of human mismanagement. Some problem cats are the product of human ignorance, neglect, or cruelty—other times, misguided love, overindulgence, and overprotectiveness cause the misbehavior. However, in all fairness to cat owners, heredity, brain injury, and other physiological conditions can also cause misbehavior in cats. If you, as a cat owner, become better informed about the causes of neurotic and problem behavior in your pets and ways of dealing with it effectively, then there will be fewer problem cats. The result will be happier owners and happier pets.

In all studies of cat behavior problems, the most important factor is the owner-pet relationship. All members of the family fall under the term "owner," and the family's actions and attitudes can make for a good pet or an incorrigible cat.

Self-styled "animal trainers," catless relatives, friends, and neighbors are all ready and willing to provide "expert advice" on feline behavior, much of it erroneous and misleading. Fortunately, excellent advice about dealing with behavior problems is also available as a result of the combined efforts of veterinarians and animal psychologists.

Researchers agree that the most important and impressionable time in a cat's life is the socialization period between three and nine weeks of age, when the kitten needs human companionship as well as the love of her mother. An "unhappy childhood" can easily result in a cat that misbehaves and that might eventually have to be put to sleep. It is an accepted scientific fact that if a kitten has no contact with humans by 12 weeks of age, it will probably become a feral (wild) or semi-feral animal,

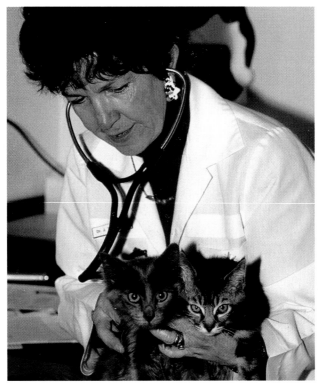

When behavior problems develop in your cat, it is important to have a veterinarian rule out any health problems that could be causing the misbehavior.

with many resultant problems.

When behavior problems develop, the obvious first step is a trip to a veterinarian for a physical checkup. If the cat's health is fine, an environmental factor might be at the root of the problem. You must recognize that you, as the owner, are the only one with the power to change the environmental factors that cause most bad habits and neuroses in your cat. You must recognize your contribution to behavior problems and your responsibility to try to correct them.

Anyone who cares for felines should realize that the growing number of pets with psychological problems and those that develop undesirable behavior for other reasons has helped create a crisis for cats. Every year, millions of homeless cats are put to death in this country. Most of them have been abandoned by their owners. Often, these owners see the cute kittens they have acquired grow into adult cats they don't like, don't want, or can't handle. In many cases, these abandoned cats are problem cats that behave in ways that are intolerable to their owners.

My chief hope is that this book will help cat owners avoid most behavior problems in their pets and deal effectively with those that do occur.

Behavioral Therapy for the Problem Cat

With the pet population increasing, and with more and more cats living in close confinement, an understanding of cats' emotional problems and how to treat them is of growing concern to the cat owner. Cats do respond to proper treatment, and it is up to each of us to find that perfect method. In severe cases in which the owner seems to be unable to help the problem cat, I recommend consulting a professional who is trained in the correction of abnormal behavior in cats.

Potentially traumatic events are inevitable in every household, and misbehaviors can result. If a cat is behaving differently and the veterinarian gives her a clean bill of health, then the owner must engage in some soul-searching. What changes have taken place in the cat's environment? Has the litter box been moved? Has the litter brand been changed? Has a strange animal come into the neighborhood? Is the cat getting into the insulation or the plant that was recently brought into the house? Is the telephone ringing too loudly or the old furnace making too much noise? What about the construction on the house next door?

Questions such as these could fill a volume, but each one is important. Are your expectations of the cat's behavior realistic? For example, a young kitten should be prevented from nibbling on your hand or ankle, but this nibbling is more likely a display of affection than of aggression. And nobody should expect a cat to maneuver gracefully around antique glass and other valuables. Some cats are exceedingly clumsy, as are most kittens prior to mature muscle development. Although human IQ tests do not apply to cats, differences in mental acuity do exist, and some cats may affectionately be labeled "retarded." These cats may look handsome, wise, and regal as long as they are stationary, but this image is shattered when they attempt that short jump from couch to coffee table and miss. Additionally, they may never learn that they can only walk uninterrupted on the kitchen counter during the owner's absence.

Experts in the U.S. estimate that there are close to six million "bad" cats—that is, cats that are overaggressive or have elimination problems. Some owners of such cats have their pets put to sleep, while many well-meaning owners just grit their teeth and suffer through the problems. The most responsible owners consult veterinarians and animal behavior specialists to help seek solutions. Cats can be retrained, and you *can* teach old cats new tricks. I have had patients as old as 12 or 13 years of age whose misbehaviors were corrected with proper retraining procedures.

Whether a cat is merely temperamental or just plain nasty, her owner usually loves her anyway. However, sometimes a mean cat's behavior goes over the line of acceptability, and reprimands and rehabilitation are in order. But a commitment is a commitment, and you don't just discard cats when they "go bad," just as you wouldn't abandon your children. Both kids and cats need guidance to get them back on the right track.

Cat training is about both resolving unwanted behavior and developing good behavior. In the rehabilitation of problem behavior in cats, exercise, diet, and environment are important considerations. Specific behavior modification therapies and possible prescription of drugs are also part of the treatment process.

Pet and Owner Conflict

If an improper technique has been used to correct a misbehavior and has actually increased the bad conduct, ill will between pet and owner can arise. Quite understandably, the owner's feelings toward the animal may change, because it is very difficult for an owner to remain affectionate toward an animal that may inflict wounds or increase housecleaning chores. Sometimes a cat keeps engaging in a certain initial misbehavior and other misbehaviors unnecessarily develop. It usually takes a lengthy process of retraining to stop the misbehaviors and to restore trust and affection in both the owner and the animal. Proper retraining methods are crucial.

Owner Motivation

Misbehaviors will undoubtedly persist in any cat despite accurate diagnosis if the owner fails to implement a professional's recommended retraining procedures. While this failure may be due to any number of factors, not the least of which is a confused interpretation of the instructions, it is most often a function of the owner's inability or refusal to expend the effort required in rehabilitation. The strength of the owner's motivation is the most important factor in the successful resolution of problem behaviors. Unfortunately, some owners are all talk and no action. Any person who acquires a pet automatically becomes responsible for care and training. Behavioral disorders in cats place demands on the owners. Responsible cat owners meet these demands.

The Importance of Playtime

In the rehabilitation of misbehaving cats, playing with your cat helps human and feline alike. It is a very relaxing and enjoyable experience. Scientists have proved that playing

Playing with your cat is more effective than any tranquilizer in normalizing your cat's temperament.

Pet and Stranger Conflict

It is important to remember that you can't force a cat on people. The cat will accept a person only if she feels secure. If the person is too noisy or handles animals too roughly, the cat will avoid that person. TLC and desensitization are needed to accustom the cat to the person or object that makes her uncomfortable.

In order to help a cat feel relaxed with a particular person, allow that person to attempt to feed her. The cat won't trust the person at first, but little by little the person can try to get closer to the cat, talking soothingly with a choice tidbit in hand. I have found that the words "kitty, kitty, kitty" in a high-pitched voice work wonders in helping someone make friends with a strange cat. In the beginning, a trusted person, with the stranger at his side, should do the feeding. Finally, when the cat will allow it, let the stranger feed the cat all by himself.

with your pet can lower your blood pressure. However, the cat receives the primary benefits from the interaction, both physically and emotionally. She loves to pretend during play that she is attacking an enemy. To pounce on "prey" is a big lift to an indoor cat that never hunts outside. The bond between owner and cat will be strong, because the playtime you share with your cat is a form of communication. If your cat is misbehaving, she will still look forward to these periods of fun and eventually, with the combination of proper retraining sessions, she will be on the path to good behavior.

Do not just throw toys on the floor and expect your cat to swat them and amuse herself. Socializing with you is what she craves. One toy that cats love that requires very little activity on your part is a laser pointer. Shine the laser on the wall or floor—most cats will enjoy trying to catch the light.

Playing with your cat is more effective than any tranquilizer in normalizing your cat's temperament. It is best to play with your cat when there is no one else around. She will be more relaxed and uninhibited in a one-on-one interaction. Play with your cat at least 15 minutes every day to use up her excess energy. After all, she has been waiting all day for you to return. It is important, however, that these games are merely fun and that none teach her to be aggressive. If she gets too rough, a sharp "no" or a flick of your finger across her nose will slow her down and teach her good manners at the same time. Remember that cats love to be gently stroked on the head and face but do not like to be rubbed on the rump or on the belly. Stroking these areas might cause some cats to strike out defensively.

Retraining Therapy

Success in retraining a cat is achieved much faster if you constantly reward the cat with food, praise, and petting. By doing this you reinforce the good behavior. Eventually, the cat will associate good behavior with direct compensation. It has been proven that using gentle words together with treats works much better than using either method by itself. Cats are very adaptable and seize on any opportunity to benefit themselves.

The Calming Response

This method is very useful in calming a nervous cat during the retraining process, or for that matter, whenever a temporary period of relaxation is needed. It evokes a gentling response in the cat, because she feels completely secure while held in the palms of her owner. For this reason, this method works best if it is the owner and not a stranger who is

holding the cat. The owner first rubs the cat's ears and chin while talking to her softly. He then very gently covers the cat's head (eyes and ears included) with the palms of his hands in the manner that one would hold an orange, without squeezing or exerting pressure. Within seconds, the cat calms down and stays that way as long as she is held in this manner. The cat relaxes due to the smell and warmth of her owner's hands as well as the partial blocking of her auditory and visual senses.

Retraining works best if a behavior is consistently rewarded. Intermittent rewarding for good behavior is confusing to a cat and does not lead to as good a result as continuous food and petting. However, once the good behavior ritual is firmly impressed on the cat's mind, the reward does not have to be given every time the cat complies. Eventually, just a kind word of endearment will suffice.

Once a misbehavior has been eradicated by retraining, it is important that the owner ensure that the cat is never again exposed to whatever prompted her to misbehave in the first place. For instance, one cat I treated would jump on the kitchen table whenever there was food on it. In order to correct this bad habit, his owner did not allow him in the kitchen. After months of good behavior, the owner allowed the cat in the kitchen again, thinking that he was cured. Not so. His first time in the kitchen, he jumped up on the table looking for food. The lesson is, do not expose the offender to temptation, no matter how long a time has passed. Cats have a long memory. The proper way of rehabilitating this cat would have been to teach him not to jump up on the table in the first place. Booby traps, such as upside-down mousetraps used cautiously, and electronic devices on the table when he was young would have been more effective and more permanent.

Preventing a misdeed is preferable to treatment after the fact, especially if the misbehavior is already ingrained in the cat's mind. It is up to the owner to anticipate the cat's next unacceptable move and stop it if possible. For instance, putting mothballs around a plant or spraying it with foul-smelling liquid or

After retraining your misbehaving cat, do not expose her to temptation. A cat that has learned to stop jumping up on the kitchen counter can still be lured anytime by the smell of yummy "people food."

hot pepper sauce is a good way to prevent trouble. The cat will remember the smell and taste of the pepper sauce and steer clear of the off-limits object.

Desensitization

To desensitize a cat, you expose the feline to a stress-inducing situation, gradually increasing the amount of annoyance until the cat doesn't react with bad behavior. While intensifying the aggravating circumstances, food rewards are in order if the cat doesn't respond to the stressor during the desensitization process. For example, if you were to attempt to overcome a cat's fear of thunderstorms, you would have her listen to recordings of storms, low at first, then with slowly increasing volume. You would reward her as her tolerance increased.

Positive and Negative Reinforcement

While negative reinforcement is very helpful in retraining naughty cats, positive reinforcement is far more effective, primarily in the form of food, but also in the form of petting and attention. Unfortunately, some misguided owners reinforce their cats' misbehavior by teaching them to be obnoxious. For instance, a cat that knocks objects off a counter is looking for attention. When you chase her, it just teaches her to do it again whenever she wants to be noticed.

If an owner ignores a continuing misbehavior, it reinforces a bad habit that can become ingrained and difficult to eradicate. For instance, when a cat continually jumps on the kitchen table to eat food, she is receiving a pleasurable reward, and the misdeed will continue indefinitely.

Treating with Tranquilizers

In the treatment of unruly cats, tranquilizers are helpful, along with behavior modification and environmental changes. Medication is not the answer for correcting most behavior problems, especially not by itself. However, tranquilizers play an important role in veterinary medicine and especially in handling and quieting nervous and neurotic cats.

For years, veterinarians have prescribed psychoactive drugs such as Valium for animals. However, new antidepressants are now available specifically for animal behavior problems. Antidepressant drugs are not always effective in treating problems, but there are some that are useful in combating spraying, howling, inappropriate urination, and aggression in cats. Your veterinarian will decide which drug is best for treating your cat's particular problem. All of these drugs are potent and must be used carefully under the supervision of a veterinarian.

Tranquilizers are useful in calming cats that are fearful of storms, strangers, cars, firecrackers, or guns. They are helpful to the female cat (queen) undergoing false pregnancy and can help overcome her anxiety about the "missing" kittens. They are also potentially indicated for treating the shy queen, to overcome her fears of the male during mating. They may help the nervous queen when she is giving birth and help prevent a refusal to nurse her kittens. Tranquilizers are also prescribed for the queen that has been known to kill her kittens. Of course, this type of cat should not be bred in the first place. There are many other uses for these drugs in the treatment of physical and emotional problems in cats.

Nevertheless, tranquilizers are not a permanent cure for any behavior problem. They represent an in-between treatment until proper rehabilitation can be initiated. You must concern yourself primarily with discovering the cause of the problem, and in most cases that in itself will lead to the cure.

With the proper retraining methods and the use of positive or negative reinforcement, most behavior problems can be prevented, eradicated, or curtailed. The procedures for raising a healthy, trouble-free animal need not mean hours of drudgery. Basically, you need to know your cat well. Training procedures and enjoyment go hand-in-hand. In fact, playtime with your cat is an ideal situation for teaching the limits of scratching, chewing, and nipping, and the lessons are fun. This very personal contact between owner and pet is the key to making behavior adjustments. Misbehaviors do develop under the best of conditions, but most can be successfully resolved with professional guidance, a little common sense, some time, and knowledge of why things went wrong. It is important to remember that rewards for good behavior are more effective than verbal or physical punishment in retraining your cat. Most cats want to please their owners because they know their owners love them.

Cats can be incredibly persistent if they are rewarded even once for misdeeds such as begging for tidbits from the dinner table. Consistent reinforcement of the household rules is vital.

How to Punish Naughty Cats

It must be evident by now that it is impossible to have a thoroughly happy, well-behaved cat without a lot of love, understanding, and a certain amount of discipline. Essentially, disciplining your cat means teaching good manners. Patience, kindness, words of praise, and a treat will work wonders in discipline and training, but it is futile to expect instant obedience from any cat. Cats generally respond to a command only when it is convenient, fun, or profitable.

Do note that when a cat's problem is caused by stress, punishment is not effective in treatment. In fact, the wrong punishment method could actually increase the stress. This chapter will discuss some of the most effective methods of punishment, but it's important to bear in mind that removing the cause of the misbehavior, whether it is stress, illness, or something else, is the best way to cure the problem.

Learning to Avoid Punishment

Owners have to be very persistent in curing cats of bad habits, because cats are very good at observational learning. They quickly learn how to avoid punishment. When punishing an animal, you should never be too harsh. Be firm, be persistent, but also show love and praise when the animal responds in a positive way.

A cat learns very quickly that *you* are holding a water pistol or squirt gun and that *you* are going to wet her, so she won't misbehave. This doesn't work. She figures out that you are the source of the punishment. You have to find a way to outwit your cat so she doesn't know where the punishment is coming from.

Also, punishing a cat after the fact for a misbehavior can create a stressful condition. Cats associate punishment with what they are doing at the time of the reprimand. It is difficult for them to read your mind and know they are being punished for some misdeed they did an hour or two before.

Things You'll Need

It is best never to strike your cat, because you will teach her nothing by it. The only thing it will do is make her afraid of you, and cats do not forgive that easily. She will avoid you whenever she can. Something that does works well is a light thump on the nose while saying "no." This gesture reminds the cat of her mother's early discipline, so the offender will associate it with a misdeed.

One of the best implements for cat punishment is your hands. You don't use them to strike the animal but clap them together to make a loud noise, at the same time saying "no" in a firm voice. Hitting your hand with a rolled-up newspaper will also scare the offender.

Grabbing a cat by the scruff of her neck and shaking her is a form of punishment that a cat understands because of her mother's discipline when she misbehaved as a kitten. However, do not lift a cat up solely by her neck and let her dangle. It's unsafe and cruel. Put one hand under her rear parts while you shake her gently.

Some other household objects are great to have around when you are planning a retraining program for your cat:

- Water Spray Cats hate water in their faces, so squirting water is a harmless but very effective form of punishment. You can use water pistols, water sprayers, or any other similar tool.
- Air Gun, Hair Dryer These can be used to blow air in a cat's face, which all cats hate. Air is a good substitute for sprays of water when you don't want to wet an area. The hissing sound of air also helps subdue a belligerent feline. With a water sprayer or air gun, the cat doesn't develop a fear of the owner himself but more of the water or air in her face.
- Aerosol Hair Spray Never spray hair spray directly on the cat's face, just in the vicinity to provide a good scare. The cat will also get to dislike the smell of the aerosol spray and will begin to associate it with punishment. Also, when the cat is out of the room, spray a scratched object or soiled area, such as a piece of furniture, rug, or curtain, with the same aerosol mist. The cat will remember the smell of the spray and begin to stay away from the object and the smell. Some ingenious owners have contrived to install a remote-controlled hair sprayer to go off whenever the cat meows excessively, especially in the middle of the night.
- Commercial Punishment Sprays One new spray designed specifically for pets allows you to interrupt the misbehaving cat with a loud rattling noise (a shaker ball in the can) and a simultaneous aroma of citronella. The combination of the two punishments is extremely effective.
- Rattling Can Filled with rocks or dry cat food, a can makes a loud noise when thrown in the direction of the misbehaver.
- Balloons These are good to tape to furniture when you are trying to keep cats away from it. If a cat accidentally bursts a balloon, the noise will leave quite an impression on her. She won't jump on or scratch the furniture if she sees a balloon there again.
- Mousetraps These traps are very impressive because they scare the cat, and she will remember the area as off-limits. It is important to turn the mousetrap upside down and replace it carefully so it does not hurt the cat when it goes off. You can also cover the trap with a newspaper to further confuse the animal. After a cat is deterred once from invading a specific area, you can

leave an unset mousetrap nearby as a reminder of the scare.

- **Double-Sticky Tape** This tape keeps a cat from walking on or scratching an off-limits surface. Cats hate to get sticky stuff on their paws. Shelf or contact paper turned sticky-side-up also works well.
- **Ping-Pong Balls** To stop undesirable behavior while the cat is in the act, you can throw ping-pong balls, which will scare the cat rather than hurt her.
- **Shock Mats** A commercial shock mat gives a mild electric shock when touched. These mats are especially useful for keeping cats off furniture, tables, and countertops. Because they offer an extreme form of punishment, they should only be used in extreme cases of misbehavior.
- **Electronic Motion Sensors** More modern sophisticated weaponry includes motion-sensor burglar alarms that set off a scary sound when the area is entered. Also, there are various other electronic gadgets that detect pressure or motion and are useful in outwitting our canny feline friends.

PUNISHING KITTENS

The use of correctional devices of any kind (water sprayer, shaker cans, etc.) is not recommended for cats under four months of age. Only positive reinforcements should

Kittens less than four months of age should never be punished with water sprayers, shaker cans, or other corrective devices. These methods are likely to aggravate inappropriate behavior in very young cats.

be used during this period, including food, praise, petting, and playtime. If corrective devices are used on very young cats, they are more likely to aggravate inappropriate behavior than to help get rid of it.

Scolding

When scolding, remember that a cat doesn't actually understand your words. He mainly responds to your actions in combination with your tone of voice. Do not be harsh, even though you scold. Use a firm tone of voice and adopt an attitude of teaching.

A scolding is important when working to get rid of a bad behavioral problem, but teaching the cat the right way is the objective. Don't let your cat grow up in an environment of hitting, slapping, yelling, screaming, and general abuse. Attempt to foster love and respect in his attitude toward you.

When scolding a cat, it is important to remember that a cat relies on her hearing more than on her sight. In fact, cats possess one of the most acute senses of hearing in the entire animal kingdom. Cats' ability to hear high-pitched sounds exceeds even that of dogs. Knowing that your cat has such sensitive hearing puts a burden of responsibility on you to keep screaming and shouting to a minimum. Trying to change your cat's behavior by screaming at him will only make matters worse.

One method of scolding that appeals to many cat lovers is the gentle approach. Some cats will stop misbehaving in response to their owner's affectionate talking, while more angry, noisy methods have no effect at all.

Introduction to Training

The Gentle Approach

If your cat is misbehaving, try a gentle and soft approach of holding and stroking her while talking gently and soothingly to her, explaining her sinful ways. You will see that your cat will respond to affection. She wants attention and for you to touch her in the same way that her mother fondled her when she was a blind little kitten.

If your cat scratches you, don't hit her back. Figure out what caused her to scratch you. Did you invite the scratch by playing too roughly with her? If you did, talk it over with her and explain to her that you meant no harm.

When you approve of your cat's behavior, tell her so in a soft, soothing voice that will show her that you love her. Cats will get the message by the tone of your voice even though they don't understand the words.

Remote Punishment

Remote punishment is often the best training method to use, because the cat doesn't see you administering the discipline. It is important that the cat in no way associate you with this discipline. The most effective means of punishment is that with which the owner is only indirectly involved.

This type of punishment should consist of a loud noise or a spray of water. Loud noises are especially unpleasant to cats. The loud swat of a rolled-up newspaper against the palm of your hand, a loud whistle, or even the clap of your hands can make a big impression on the cat caught in a misbehavior. You can sneak around and follow the cat, and when she looks like she's going to misbehave, you can throw a noisy object in her direction, such as a can filled with stones. You don't hit the cat, just scare her with the noise. You can also throw nuts in the shell, rubber balls, or anything else that won't hurt the cat but is noisy. Cats are very frightened of anything flying through the air in their direction. After that, talk gently to the cat and reassure her that you still love her while you scratch her ears. After several experiences of objects flying at her, she will generally get the idea.

However, one cannot always be around when the offender is engaging in her inappropriate action. This is the time to use upside-down mousetraps, balloons, and electronic gadgets as implements in remote punishment. Once she has learned her lesson, you can gradually remove the mousetraps or whatever else you were using to deter her. Just leaving an

Remote punishment.

The "time-out" method is effective with cats as well as children. Place the cat in a small room or cage immediately after the infraction so that the cat knows why she is being punished.

uncocked mousetrap or a water gun on the off-limits object will usually remind her of the consequences.

"Time-Out" Method

The "time-out" method works well with children, and it is very effective in disciplining cats. Whenever a cat misbehaves, put her in a small room or cage by herself for a while. The length of time should be regulated by the severity of the infraction and how long you have been trying to retrain the cat. The banishment has to be accomplished immediately after the infraction so that the cat will know why she is being punished. If you put her in the bathroom, which is a good room to use, be sure to remove the toilet

Remove the toilet paper when using the "time-out" method in the bathroom.

21

paper because some irate cats will rebel and tear up all the paper they can find. This time-out method is good to use if a cat wakes you in the middle of the night. After being confined two or three times, she will begin to realize that she will be put away if she wakes you up.

Final Word on Punishment

Physical punishment is not only cruel, it will get you nowhere, and you most likely will never be forgiven. Cats do not forgive and forget easily, and because cats have long memories, you must above all be consistent in your requests, responses, and methods so as not to confuse or deceive them. Complimenting cats on their good behavior yields better results than scolding them for their transgressions. Raving and ranting noisily at a cat does not make any impression on her feline brain. The owner may feel better letting off steam, but he's likely to make the behavior worse. Hitting a cat often leads to exactly the opposite of what the owner intends–increased and worse misbehaviors.

Hitting your cat is not only cruel, it will get you nowhere, and you most likely will never be forgiven.

BEHAVIOR MODIFICATION

We've all heard the expression "You can't teach an old dog new tricks," but what about an old cat—or a young one, for that matter?

The answer to the question is yes, you can. Although it can be too early to start training (except for housebreaking and scratching), it is never too late. You *can* train cats, but you cannot train them as you train dogs. They do not respond as consistently to commands as dogs do, and getting them to conform to your wishes is tough. A cat has a mind of her own. You have to accept the fact that a cat is independent and a rugged individualist.

The good news is, if you play your cards right, it'll be easier than you think to modify your cat's behaviors. That's because cats communicate on a very high level with their owners, verbally and nonverbally. While dogs make only 40 sounds, cats make more than 100 sounds on a regular basis. In fact, cats possess one of the largest spoken vocabularies of all the animals in the animal kingdom, including gorillas and chimpanzees.

So before you embark on any behavior modification program, it's up to you to learn how to communicate with your cat. It is not the cat's responsibility to understand us, but our obligation to understand them. Communication with a cat is a two-way street. If you can establish communication, you are in for some extraordinary and rewarding experiences. No, it's not necessary or possible to know the whole range of your cat's vocabulary, but it is necessary to be able to understand her basic messages about what's going on in her life. These messages are your key to understanding your cat's physical and emotional states at any given time. Familiarity with them allows you to determine what is causing a behavior and what you should do about it.

Talking to your cat helps to establish a strong relationship between the two of you. In fact, many experts believe talking is the single most important factor in forming a good relationship between cat and owner and that it is very important when you are working to bring about desired changes in behavior.

What is Behavior Modification?

As the name implies, behavior modification involves changing behaviors from unacceptable to acceptable. Giving or withholding rewards can change behavior. The

Cats need to scratch—it's one behavior that is just part of being a cat.

concept of behavior modification developed when laboratory studies showed that an animal would respond to a certain stimulus in a predictable way if his response behavior was reinforced. That is, when the animal was put in the same stimulating situation more than once, his response would be the same as before if he associated that response with receiving a reward. Also, his response would be the same each time if he associated a stimulating situation with the avoidance of pain or the avoidance of something unpleasant, such as not receiving a reward.

From these early experiments, behavioral scientists realized that reinforcement can have a powerful effect on learning. Many of the current child-rearing practices are based on this concept.

Behavior modification works exceptionally well with animals, because it provides a means of communicating that the animal will understand. A good response is followed by a reward, and a bad response is followed by a punishment (which can simply be the lack of a reward). A cat can understand this and will learn to respond with good behavior.

Reinforcement

Reinforcement is the key to success with this type of therapy. Positive reinforcement is praise, petting, or a tasty tidbit to nibble—a kind word or caress that can make the cat feel that she is pleasing her owner. Negative reinforcement could mean a sharp scolding, a flick of a finger on the nose, or in drastic cases, isolation, as in the time-out method. Other implements of punishment can be water or air sprays, electronic scare tactics, etc.

Types Of Behavior

There are three types of behaviors that need to be considered when we talk about behavior modification. They include those that a cat manifests because normal cat instincts are at work, those that a cat engages in only under stressful situations, and those that are simply bad habits. Behaviors in this last group—bad habits—can and should be corrected by behavior modification. Those in the other two groups may not be eradicable, but they can at least be modified. Let's look at these two categories first.

It's Just Part Of Being A Cat

There are some behaviors that you must not stop altogether, like scratching. Cats need to scratch; that's how they remove the outer sheath of the claws on their front feet to make room for new growth underneath. A cat's scratching is not meant to be destructive, nor is your cat doing it to get on your nerves. Scratching is an essential form of exercise for your cat.

Cats also need to climb—it is an essential part of any cat's life. Being unable to climb causes confusion and frustration. That's not to say that you can't train your cat to climb only on certain pieces of furniture. This is where behavior modification techniques can work to your advantage.

Neutering can eliminate many normal-but-negative feline behaviors. You may have an intact male cat that is so preoccupied with his sexual desires that his behaviors become unbearable. No amount of behavior modification will change these

All cats love and need to climb, although they can be trained to climb only on certain pieces of furniture.

circumstances. An intact female cat has her own set of sexual frustrations when she is in heat, resulting in negative behaviors that you won't be able to modify, either. She'll be too nervous to show any affection toward you. Worse, she'll be so nervous that she'll sometimes forget how to use the litter box.

ONE STRESSED-OUT CAT

Cats are really no different from their owners. What causes stress in our lives can easily cause stress in our cats' lives too. Don't think for a moment that changes in our routines and lifestyles—a marital breakup, job uncertainty, a death in the family—aren't going to have a behavioral impact on our furry companions. Suddenly, we notice they're behaving in ways we've never seen before, and we don't like what we see. Then there are the typical cat stresses, like a visit to the vet's office or even prolonged exposure to noise.

With stress-related problems, a slightly different form of behavior modification is necessary. After all, we know that the behaviors we want to modify are not nonstop, although if left unchallenged, they can last longer than necessary.

In these situations, preventive measures are extremely effective. For example, always talk to your cat and prepare her for any surprises. If there's going to be a change in your cat's environment, remove her from that environment and keep her in a room where no change is taking place.

If the whole family is moving, introduce your cat to her new surroundings by putting her in a room that has familiar furniture in it as well as her litter box, food, water, and toys. This means that you must remember to pack Kitty's essentials separately and have them readily available. Also make sure your cat gets some extra loving attention during any stressful adjustment period.

Is Your Cat Really Bad?

Once you have separated the behaviors that you consider negative but still acceptable, you need to designate the negative behaviors that are not acceptable. You need to determine whether your cat falls into the "bad cat" category. Here's how to tell:

Count the number of times you say "no" to your cat, or "stop that," or "get away from there." Now count how many times you say "yes," "good kitty," or "atta boy."

Unfortunately, most of us have a tendency to pay more attention to the negative behaviors our cats exhibit, and in the process we make two very big mistakes. When we see our cat doing something wrong, we have a tendency to shout and grab her, and we generally do it incorrectly—holding her under her armpits so that her shoulders are pressed uncomfortably against her cheeks and her heavy hindquarters are dangling awkwardly.

The worst part of all this is that you're so busy paying attention to the negative that you ignore the positive, and this is what happens: Your cat starts interpreting punishment as reward. Being punished is the only way she gets attention, and attention is what she wants. After all, you're her mother. No matter how old your cat is, she still sees you as her pseudo-parent, so she acts and thinks like a kitten when she's around you. Whether you're male or female, you're your cat's mother. She's looking to you for lots of TLC, for unconditional love. She knows you can't do things like her real mother did, such as lick her all over, but she's willing to make some compromises. In your case,

When we see our cats doing something wrong, we have a tendency to shout and grab them, and we generally hold them incorrectly when we're angry.

When punishment is the only attention a cat receives, she will start misbehaving in order to be noticed by her owner.

she'll go for stroking instead of licking. (Did you ever notice how every time you stroke your cat, she sticks her tail up? It's a throwback to her days with her real mother; an invitation for Mom to examine her anal region.)

Accentuate the Positive, Eliminate the Negative

I recommend that you begin behavior modification by working on just one bad behavior. While some experts say that this behavior should be the worst one, I recommend just the opposite—the least unacceptable behavior. As far as I'm concerned, success breeds success, and if you start out with the least disruptive behavior, chances are you'll be successful faster. As you advance to the more problematic behaviors, your furry friend and you will be used to the "program." The program is simple: *reward positive behavior and ignore negative behavior.* The hard part is taking the time to make it work. Rewarding positive behavior is generally more time-consuming than punishing negative behavior. Behavior change doesn't happen overnight. It also takes a lot more self-restraint to ignore negative behavior.

Behavior modification with cats works on a very basic principle. We know that cats like attention; they'll take it however they can get it. If you only pay attention to your cat when he's doing something wrong, the punishment becomes the reward. If you ignore the negative behavior, the absence of attention becomes the punishment. If in addition to ignoring the negative behavior you pay attention when your cat behaves admirably—Bingo!

Now for the rewards. What does your cat like? Catnip or other delicacies can be used as positive reinforcers, because bribery does work in a cat. If your cat engages in positive behavior—i.e., the opposite of the negative behavior you're trying to minimize, you give her a taste of catnip. Just don't overdo it. It's not that a cat will become addicted, it's just that she will get so used to it she will lose interest and it will no longer have any effect. There are many other juicy morsels that may be used as rewards for good behavior.

Giving your cat attention by holding her, petting her, and cuddling her can be one of the best rewards. Make sure you are willing to commit to the time it takes to focus on your cat when she demonstrates the positive behaviors you are working toward.

Self-Image and Behavior Modification

Because your cat considers the relationship she has with you so important, her self-image is intricately linked to your relationship. In other words, whether your cat has a positive or negative self-image depends on how you address your cat's positive and negative behaviors. Your cat will live up or down to your expectations. Tell your cat how naughty she has been, and your cat will feel very bad, even embarrassed, so don't be surprised if she doesn't come scampering to the door when you get home. Worse, don't be surprised if she really starts exhibiting negative behavior patterns. After all, she wouldn't want to disappoint you. If she thinks you think she's bad, she'll be bad.

Even though you may think your cat takes great pleasure in driving you crazy, she may not think she's doing anything wrong. She may be taking all her cues from you. The more times you let her know what a "bad kitty" she is, the more she'll start believing you. After all, "mother knows best."

As you put behavior modification into practice, ignoring negative behaviors and rewarding positive behaviors, your cat's negative self-image will begin to change. The best way to develop a positive self-image in your cat is to give positive reinforcement for the things your cat does well. Besides, if you don't reward your cat for her good behavior, how will she ever know what good behavior is? In all attempts at behavior modification, patience is essential. Do not attempt to change your cat's behavior at a faster pace than she can accommodate. Considerable repetition of a procedure will reinforce the cat's ability to change.

The more times you tell your cat what a "bad kitty" she is, the more she'll believe you.

Normal Cat Behavior

I n order to better understand problem cats and how they differ from normal cats, let us first look briefly at the behavior, instinct, intelligence, and personality of a normal cat.

Although I suspect that many cats, like many people, might resent being labeled "normal," I use the term as a convenient catchall phrase describing the characteristics of well-adjusted cats with generally desirable behavior. But remember, what is desirable behavior in one situation may be undesirable in another. The term "normal" encompasses a variety of temperaments, habits, and idiosyncrasies, even among cats of the same breed.

For similar convenience, I use the term "abnormal" for those cats that are not well adjusted and that are chronic misbehavers. Fortunately, these problem cats can be helped. When the bad behavior is caused, wholly or partially, by mental or emotional disorders, I use the term "neurotic" to describe it. Neurotic cats are more difficult to help and need lots more patience and care for rehabilitation.

The normal cat, that model companion we all hope to see realized in the pets we love, is a self-assured cat who is outgoing and friendly with people and other cats and possesses a fine pride in his own intelligence. He will greet guests, but he is neither overly friendly nor shy. He will not scratch, bite, or fight except to protect himself, his food, or his mate. He is well adjusted, because he has no personality traits that have to be corrected. The normal cat is usually a happy cat. A happy cat is the product of mutual cooperation between owner and pet.

A normal, happy cat.

A properly reared kitten is naturally sociable and eager to make friends. She desires gentle handling, responds favorably to people, and grows up without experiencing fear. After weaning, a kitten should be gently handled by strangers so that she may learn that there are other gentle human beings outside her family. An animal learns by association and repetition. The more often it is exposed to tenderness and love, the more favorable will be its impression of humans. A kitten's basic instinct is to love and be loved. However, if she suffers an unhappy kittenhood, her confidence in people could turn to anxiety and distrust. We then have a problem cat.

At times it is difficult to distinguish between normal and neurotic behavior in cats (or humans). A docile little pet might turn into a ferocious tiger when being groomed or during nail clipping. Under those circumstances, it would not be considered abnormal behavior if she were to scratch or bite her owner. This is a normal reaction to grooming in an untrained cat, but it is obvious that such a cat needs some training.

Cats seem to be aware of their owners' emotional ups and downs and will react accordingly. Cats are also very sensitive to the physical well-being of their owner. If a person doesn't feel well, either emotionally or physically, a cat can detect the situation and may want to be close to that person to help comfort him or her. If their favorite humans are under stress, cats may behave as if they, too, are stressed.

Distinctive Breed Behaviors

Certain breeds have distinct inherited physical and behavioral characteristics. However, there are many behavioral differences within each breed itself, because most cats are independent individuals and do as they please. The following characteristics are generalities and cover the majority in each breed. It is important to remember that there are exceptions in every breed and you may encounter many rugged individualists that behave according to their own whims. Virtually all the breeds can be described as intelligent and affectionate. However, a closer analysis of the breeds shows that, generally speaking, they are different in personality:

ORIENTAL BREEDS

Siamese:	Outgoing, loyal, intolerant of other cats, and fearful of young children
Abyssinian:	Sweet-tempered, obedient
Somali:	Shy, easy-going
Burmese:	Very affectionate, loves to be in the company of people

LONG-HAIRED BREEDS

Persian:	For the most part, calm, even-tempered, gentle, and quiet, while some are even sweet-natured. Some are more outgoing and inquisitive than others. Most are affectionate.
Himalayan:	Likes people, much quieter than the Siamese
Angora:	Friendly, gentle
Maine Coon:	Likes people, good companion

Normal Cats

Birman:	Likes people, docile
Balinese:	Much quieter than the Siamese
Ragdoll:	Easy to get along with

SHORT-HAIRED BREEDS

Shorthairs tolerate handling more than some breeds such as Siamese. All of these cats demand attention, some more than others.

American Shorthair:	In general they are energetic, robust, and hardy. Most are good-natured, even-tempered, and friendly
Russian Blue:	A quiet, shy cat
Korat:	Good-natured
Tonkinese:	Loves people, very affectionate
Rex:	Very playful
Egyptian Mau:	Very obedient, will learn tricks
Bombay:	Loves people, not happy when left alone

The Oriental breeds are the most active, while long-haired breeds are least active. Short-haired cats are more friendly, while Oriental cats are less friendly, the Abyssinians the least friendly. Oriental breeds are more destructive than Shorthairs. Persians are least destructive. Siamese, Burmese, and Abyssinian are the most vocal, while Persians are the least vocal. Siamese are the most playful, while Persians are the least playful. Siamese (followed by Burmese and Abyssinian) are most excitable. Shorthairs and Persians are equally calm. All cats keep themselves fairly clean, but Persians less so.

A female cat's maternal instinct is so strong that she may adopt toys or other objects as "kittens," lavishing them with affection and never letting them out of her sight.

A "Mother's" Undying Love

Some cats never lose their maternal instinct, no matter how old they get. One case in point is that of a five-year-old cat, Squeaky, who had a fixation with a cat toy that peeped whenever it was handled. She carried this stuffed toy with her wherever she went. She kept it beside her when she slept. They were inseparable. One day, her owners brought home a kitten, and it was love at first sight. Squeaky forgot about the toy "kitten" and immediately showered all of her affection on the new, live addition. She cared for the kitten as if it were her own. The stuffed toy was a thing of the past. She had a *real* kitten to look after.

Normal Instincts

Your cat has many curious and unique instincts that are legacies from her wild ancestry. In reality, you have a breath of the wild in your home, still retaining traces of the days when your cat's ancestors roamed the woods, matching wits with prey and predators. H. H. Monroe Lamb, a famous philosopher, said that the cat is the only animal that has adapted to civilization without losing any of its feral instincts.

Maternal Instinct

One of the most important basic feline instincts is the maternal instinct.

The maternal instinct of a cat is, of course, a prominent factor when she is raising kittens. One of the earliest signs of this instinct is when the mother makes a nest before the onset of the birth of the kittens. The queen's licking and eating of the placenta seems to be a necessary preliminary to the cleaning of the young. It also seems to be the basis of the maternal attachment to the offspring.

Normally, the queen tends the litter and stays close for about four weeks. Then, gradually, she leaves the kittens for

The maternal instinct.

longer periods of time. She will clean the kittens by licking them and by ingesting their urine and feces until they are about six weeks old. By then, they will have been taught to use the litter box to eliminate. When they are about four weeks of age, she starts training them: She punishes them, growls at them, cuffs them, and knocks them over. She begins to lose part of the maternal bond when the kittens start taking solid food at about four weeks of age. However, the queen always retains a maternal link with her kittens if there is no interruption through separation.

One aspect of maternal behavior is the grooming instinct. Cats, especially mother cats, will sometimes engage in this advanced type of social behavior, combing for fleas, ticks, or other debris either in their young or in their human family. Some cats show affection by nibbling on their owner's arm or leg. Males do this more often; the tom also nibbles the queen's neck during the mating ritual. It is normal for male as well as female cats to "groom" someone in their human family. They will lick the ears and neck in an affectionate way, their expression of extreme love.

SUCKLING INSTINCT

The suckling instinct is a strong behavior in a kitten. If the mother does not suckle her kittens, a substitute must be provided. It is best to use a bottle with a small hole in the nipple so the kittens will have to work to get the milk. If a kitten is not allowed to suck, a non-nutritional bad habit of sucking will often develop and persist into adulthood.

KNEADING INSTINCT

The kneading instinct, or "making bread," is familiar to all cat owners. Kneading usually signifies the cat's excitement when a favorite person, another cat, a stimulating smell, or an interesting fabric texture emotionally arouses her. This instinct is first seen in newborn kittens, who knead their mother's breast to stimulate the flow of milk while sucking.

SEXUAL INSTINCT

Originally, in the wild state, cats usually were monogamous and stayed with their own mates. Today, however, male cats play the gallant to every queen in heat, even complete strangers.

Kittens, like children, have early sexual sensations and can be sexually stimulated. The mother licks her kittens, stimulating the genitals and other sensitive areas. Littermates rub against one another and their mother for pleasurable sensations. During early growth, long before sexual maturity, kittens exhibit sexual excitement during oral and bodily contact. There is no differentiation between the sexes—males ride males and females are stimulated by females. This is normal behavior for kittens.

HUNTING INSTINCT

The cat has always been a highly specialized predator, and no amount of domestication will change this instinct. Her hearing, sight, retractable claws, strength, speed, sense of balance, and homing abilities are the inbred factors that make her such a great

All cats are innate hunters. However, keeping your cats safely indoors ensures that they will never get to practice their hunting skills on anything but toys and the occasional housefly.

hunter. Your cat's favorite games simulate the natural behavior of chasing prey, catching it, and carrying it back to her lair.

Do not scold your cat when she brings you a dead bird or a baby rabbit. Most experts believe that she is actually showing you what a fine hunter she is and giving you a present. However, there is another school of thought about a cat bringing a dead animal home. Some experts believe that a cat is not bringing a gift for the owner, but is simply coming to a place where she can eat in privacy and safety. These experts say that if you approach the cat, she will run away with your "gift." However, I have seen a cat walk proudly into the house with a mouse between her teeth and lay the victim at the feet of her owner. It probably depends on the mood of the cat at the time. She might just want to brag about her hunting skills, especially after having her fill of several of her victims.

Hunting is a good example of learned behavior. A mother cat teaches her young kittens to hunt by bringing small prey to the litter, and as they get older, she will take them on hunting expeditions. A good hunter teaches her kittens how to stalk and swoop down on their prey efficiently. Kittens born to queens that are not hunters are less likely to become hunters themselves. So if a mother cat is a hunter, you might try removing the kittens from the litter before the hunting age arrives, which is at about eight weeks.

Killing Birds

This is a serious concern for some cat owners. However, punishment is not effective, because the desire to hunt is instinctive. Throwing things at or hitting your cat does not deter her from hunting. The best way of dealing with the problem is prevention. The most commonly used preventive device is a bell attached to the cat's collar. However, there are some ingenious cats that can still catch birds even with bells on. Some cats can be taught not to attack birds through a retraining program, which requires lots of time and patience. By using toy birds that look and sound like the real thing, you can teach the cat not to go after any bird. You can booby-trap the toy bird with a bad-tasting and foul-smelling substance, or you can attach an electronic device that will scare the cat if she goes too close to the decoy. Repetition over a period of time will inhibit even an expert bird killer.

HOMING INSTINCT

When hunting for food for her young, the outdoor cat must be able to find her way back to her kittens. Her homing instinct is a vital part of her makeup. This instinct seems stronger in some cats than in others. It is linked to the territorial instinct and requires a sense of direction and a certain amount of sight and sound memory.

There are many reports about the homing instinct in cats that cite cases of cats returning to their old homes after traveling hundreds and even thousands of miles away. Some of this ability can be attributed to the marking of territory. Also, a cat has a built-in compass of sorts. However, behavioral scientists have investigated animal migratory capabilities, based on reports of cats that found their owners newly relocated in places where the animal had never been. Such a capability rules out the possible exercise of basic senses as well as memory. The ability is called psi-trailing, and hundreds of cases have been reported. It is clear that cats have extraordinary sensory abilities that we do not understand and cannot explain.

TERRITORIAL INSTINCT

An indoor cat usually has a favorite spot in the house. This is her particular territory, although she roams the entire house.

Outdoor cats have a home territorial range that they cover daily. Clawing or scraping bark off trees is one way that these cats show the neighborhood felines that this is their territory. Odors from the paws are transferred to the trees so that curious marauding cats know whose domain they are invading. The tree bark is further "personalized" by urination or spraying.

MARKING INSTINCT

Marking behavior is used to indicate territorial limits and is acted out as a method of communication. A cat rubs against objects to distribute her scent from glands in her skin. These are located in her chin, mouth, ears, paws, and anal and tail regions. When two cats rub against each other, they are depositing their scent on each other. When

A cat rubs against objects to distribute her scent, marking the objects as her territory. When she rubs against her owner, it is a greeting that denotes both affection and possession.

they rub against humans, it is a form of greeting behavior that denotes affection, indicating that they feel you belong to them.

Scratching is also a form of marking behavior. The appearance of scratch marks shows territorial possession to other cats. However, it should be remembered that scratching is also a cat's method of conditioning her claws.

Urine-marking is another important method of communication between cats and is seen in both males and females. Marking behavior can also result in the deposit of feces in inappropriate places.

PERCHING INSTINCT

Cats usually like to lie in high places where they can relax and sleep in comfort without having to worry about enemies. High perches also assist the cat in the hunt for prey, enabling her to survey the landscape for her next unsuspecting meal.

SCRATCHING INSTINCT

Because scratching is such a deeply ingrained instinct in cats, its distressing consequences in a house full of modern-day furniture, rugs, and draperies are all too familiar to most cat owners. Indeed, scratching is one of the most common problems faced by cat owners. No amount of scolding or punishment will make this natural tendency go away, but it can be channeled into one source with the proper training. A scratching post is one of the most successful methods of dealing with the problem.

There are many types of posts, from those that are 12 inches high to those that extend all the way to the ceiling, and they come with many variations, including those with ladders and shelves spaced along the pole. A ball or other toy attached to the post can entertain a cat for hours while allowing her to hit and scratch away all her frustrations. Other scratching devices contain catnip to capture the cat's attention.

Today's elaborate cat trees, posts, and hideaways satisfy the cat's need to perch in high places and also serve as an acceptable place to scratch.

PLAY INSTINCT

The play instinct is fascinating to most people, never more so than when it involves mock fighting, because most cats seem to know exactly when to stop. Ears are pulled, mouths are locked together, tails are ruffed, and then somebody lets out one real "yipe" and they both stop. Afterward, the fighters may even curl up and rest together.

TOILET TRAINING INSTINCT

Toilet training is a combination of instinct and learning. Cats' urge to bury their feces is instinctive, because by covering their trail they are protected from their enemies. However, the kitten learns by watching her mother scratch in the litter box and cover up her excretions.

The Language Of Cats

A cat emits an astonishing jumble of purrs, meows, growls, chirrups, wails, squawks, howls, spits, and gurgles. These sounds all signify something: anger, affection, discomfort, contentment, desire, or hunger. Cats can communicate with their eyes, ears, tails, fur—essentially, with their whole body.

The cat's tail is a barometer of her emotional ups and downs. A contented cat carries her tail high and lets it droop when she feels dissatisfied. A twitching tail is ambiguous; it may indicate either satisfaction or annoyance. When a cat wags her tail, beware. She is getting angry. Crouched low with the tail straight behind, a cat is stalking. Cats flick their tails in situations where humans would thumb their noses. A good example of this is when your cat refuses her food. She may combine jerking her tail contemptuously with scratching movements. A cat uses her tail like a chatterbox. When she sits with a group of cats, their tails will move back and forth as if the cats are gossiping with each other. When taking a cat to a "strange territory" such as somebody's house or your new home, she may approach the new area by walking low to the floor, with her tail down. After she sniffs out all corners and crevices and is convinced there is no imminent danger, her whole body will lift, including her tail.

Reading a cat's face is important. An alert cat has erect ears and narrow pupils. A frightened cat's ears flatten and her pupils widen. A relaxed cat shows her pleasure through half-closed eyes. When a cat flattens her ears against her head, she is angry. When she pricks her ears forward, she is alert and expectant.

Rubbing her whiskers against your leg shows her affection for you and also marks you as part of her territory. Arching her back with raised fur means hostility.

Purring is still a mystery. Cats largely purr when they are contented but occasionally when they are in pain. Some researchers believe the purr comes from air passing over the voice box, while others believe it comes from vibrations in the chest cavity.

It is important for us to understand the moods and gestures of cats so that we can respond to them properly. Just because you each speak different languages doesn't mean that you can't have meaningful conversations with your cat. Learn to understand the full range of your cat's communications, including body language, purring, and facial expressions. Be sure to talk back!

It's important to learn to understand your cat's body language. For example, this alert, surprised cat has erect ears and wide eyes. She is crouched low to the ground, perhaps because she is exploring a strange environment.

Personality

Just as with people, no two cats are exactly alike (even identical twin littermates). There are always differences in features, traits, temperament, personality, intelligence, and behavior.

Though you may have heard from numerous "authorities" such generalizations as "mixed breeds are smarter than pedigreed cats," none of them is true. Every degree of intelligence and every personality type can be found in every breed and mixture. Your cat's personality and intelligence depend in part on heredity and in part on the treatment she receives from you.

In a group of cats, we usually see almost every personality type and temperament: the leader and the follower, the brave, cowardly, sly, dumb, friendly, or timid cat, and, of course, the bully. The cat's personality and temperament are the sum total of physical, mental, emotional, and social characteristics as modified by instinct, experience, and training in early kittenhood. Proper training and a favorable environment usually produce a cat with a pleasant personality and an even temperament.

All cats have individual personalities that are formed between 4 and 12 weeks of age. Heredity and environment influence the personality of any individual. The way

the kitten is exposed to her surroundings during the formative period between these ages influences the way she will turn out as an adult. Bad handling by humans or other animals during this time can determine what kind of cat she will be.

After 12 weeks of age, a kitten can also be influenced by unhappy incidents but to a much smaller extent. An older kitten is much more resistant to personality change brought about by the environment.

Cats are not cold and disdainful. They thoroughly appreciate the companionship of humans and other animals. When human love is not available, they become wild. Also, contrary to popular belief, they are more attached to a person than to a place. They know when they are really loved and understood and have many ways of communicating their desires and feelings. Cats do not show affection like dogs. They are more subtle about being demonstrative. They show affection by rubbing against your ankle or hand or by purring. They love to have their ears or chins scratched. True, they are intensely self-centered. This characteristic makes them independent, self-reliant, dignified, and resourceful. People not kindly disposed to them call them disobedient, arrogant, fickle, unpredictable, and ungrateful. But they walk tall, and they are proud. They will not allow themselves to be abused or mistreated in exchange for a favor. Probably no other animal has so completely maintained its indomitable freedom and independence in its association with humans as the domestic cat has. Her devotion is voluntary and cannot be commanded.

An Extroverted Cat

In my 50-year experience with cats, I have met one particularly remarkable cat with a distinct personality of his own. He is a very unusual Abyssinian named Savannah who doesn't know he is a cat but thinks he is a "people."

Savannah loves going out with his mistress for walks and for rides around town in the family car. When his owner holds up his leash, he usually comes running with his motor purring.

Most everyone in the neighborhood appreciates Savannah and takes time to talk to and pet this lovable animal. All the local restaurants know Savannah has good table manners, and they allow him to be seated with other patrons. He is served on his own plate and eats very daintily, much to the amusement of the other diners.

Savannah loves posing for photographers and being among people. He also enjoys being around children and often visits them in classrooms. Savannah is always friendly to all people, purring and inviting them to come closer to him, impressing them with his unique personality.

Normal Cats

Intelligence

Intelligent people recognize that cats are thinking, understanding, responsive creatures of great intelligence. There is growing controversy among psychologists and cat owners over whether certain performances of cats are the result of training or indicate intelligence, reasoning power, and judgment. I am not a psychologist, but there is much evidence that convinces me that many cats have a high degree of intelligence. Psychologists contend that because cat training mostly involves repetition, cats learn only by conditioned reflexes. However, I have seen many cats show judgment by thoughtfully appraising certain situations and then carefully taking the correct course of action.

It is not fair to compare the intelligence of various species of animals. Some animals are better adapted than others to a particular terrain, climate, way of life, or role in society. For instance, cats are better adapted to tree climbing than some animals, but this cannot be considered a measure of intelligence.

In comparative tests with other animals, the cat does not rate very high because she simply will not cooperate in this type of research. The conventional intelligence test consistently underrates the cat, because the cat considers it just plain nonsense.

The cat's ability to survive in stressful environments shows a high degree of intelligence, more so than purely instinctive reaction. Even an apartment cat thrown out in the wilderness can survive the elements and predators—for a while, anyway.

There are some who maintain that cats never consciously think about their actions, but rather are motivated purely by instinct. I do not agree. Cats demonstrate their intelligence in a number of ways. They are ingenious and inventive in the use of their paws—for instance, rapping on doors, opening doors, operating gadgets, and knocking telephone receivers off the hook. Learning to cooperate with other cats in joint ventures such as hunting is also a sure sign of intelligence.

Some cats are more intelligent than others and can learn by observing the actions of people. Many of them are so smart that they can outwit their owners by watching their repetitious actions and figuring out a solution to the problem. Most cats can find out a way to hoodwink their owners. They are fast learners when they want to be.

There is a very interesting case concerning learned behavior in an orphaned kitten. He was raised by hand in a family that also had a male dog. The dog and cat were raised together and became very close friends. As the cat got older, he would only urinate by raising his rear leg against a tree like his companion. This is called observational learning.

Although cats cannot read clocks, there is no doubt that they possess the ability to know what time of day it is. At one time I lived on the top floor of a high-rise apartment building in a large city. My wife could tell the time I was to return in the evening by watching our cat, Hosea. Every day, five minutes before I was to arrive, Hosea yawned, stretched, and sauntered over to the door.

Cats also have good memories. They do not forget or forgive easily. A painful experience can be etched in a feline brain forever. For example, a person stepping on a cat's tail accidentally can occasionally turn the cat away and cause her to retain a

Cats have a very accurate internal clock. Every day, five minutes before the author was to arrive home from work, his cat Hosea would saunter over to the door to wait for him.

hatred for that person. It may take a long period of desensitization to train the cat to accept that person again.

Your intelligent cat will train you to suit her convenience. She will let you know how she likes her food and what kind of food she will eat, when she likes to be served and where, and in what part of the house she wishes to sleep. Cats can train humans amazingly well, and some humans are quick to learn.

Behavioral Influences

Behavior is never wholly inherited or totally acquired but always developed under the combined influences of heredity and environment. The goal in socializing a cat is to produce a well-balanced and well-adjusted animal. Each cat is very much an individual and should be regarded as such. If you study your cat's individual traits and reactions, you will be able to train and manage her more effectively. When you are familiar with your cat's personality and normal behavior patterns, you will be quick to notice the slightest deviations.

Research has shown that prenatal environmental influences can affect the behavior of kittens. When the mother is handled gently during pregnancy, the offspring are likely to be more docile and less easily upset by sudden disturbances in the environment. On the other hand, certain drugs given to the pregnant cat can alter the behavior of the offspring, and it has been demonstrated experimentally that administering electric shock to pregnant queens results in overexcitable kittens.

Feline Antics

In my many years of association with cats, I have always been amazed at the many ludicrous ways that cats' normal behavior can express itself. These "playing" rituals mimic the cat's ancestral behavior, which is indispensable for survival. These antics keep the owners alternately amused and frustrated, but they are a healthy way for a cat to assert herself and release her inhibitions. In short, it's important to remember that your seemingly nutty cat may be absolutely normal—in her eyes, anyway.

A Cat's-Eye View

If numbers are any indicator, 62 million household cats must be doing something right. These days, they've pretty much displaced dogs as the people's choice for a companion animal. Actually, cats do *everything* right, from the cat's point of view.

Cats don't consult books on etiquette. They don't live according to spelled-out rules of behavior. They wouldn't deign to consider themselves subservient (though sometimes they pretend to be) and, of course, guilt or shame do not even exist in their world. Besides that, cats can circumvent almost any attempts to limit their independence. (Ever notice those paw prints on the "off-limits" kitchen counter when you get home?) Basically, you might sum up a cat's attitude as, "I am who I am."

To glimpse just what that might mean, it might help to put yourself in a cat's shoes—well, her paws. Imagine, just for a moment, what it's like being able to see the tiniest movement, hear the smallest sound, be bombarded by smells, and be

Val loves to swing in a pillowcase.

so small that every intense sensation seems magnified, never mind being able to leap five times the distance of your own body length.

Most owners of my feline patients, and most cat owners in general, see their cats as undemanding, easy to care for, and a joy to watch and interact with, their antics frequently more hilarious than harmful. Take the case of Blueberry, a calico that loves to engage her owner in a daily game of "fetch," retrieving a crumpled piece of notepaper. Then there is Val, the Russian Blue that delights in being swung around in a pillowcase like a lasso.

I've also known cat owners who say they're living with "the cat from hell"— cats whose antics drive them to distraction. These cats have an attitude. They chew clothing, tear furniture to shreds, and have trouble keeping the peace with other cats or humans. A swipe at an owner's nose or claws digging into an owner's shoulders only draw blood, not raves. Before indicting the behavior of any cat, it's always a good idea first to consult a veterinarian to determine if the offending conduct, such as aggressive behavior, may actually be due to a physiological problem or disease. As a rule, though, most of what your cat does is instinctive. Her antics and quirks may take as many forms as snowflakes.

Most behaviors, though, even negative ones, begin to make sense if we try to see them from the cat's perspective, developing a "cat's-eye view" of sorts. There's usually a logical reason behind everything your cat does. Knowing what makes her tick can help you cope and understand and even increases your enjoyment of her. Consider the simplest example, like when your cat rubs her face against your leg. You may think she's just being affectionate, and that's fine; after all, why not allow your ego a boost? I hope this doesn't shatter your illusions, but what the cat actually is doing is something that comes quite naturally. She's marking you as part of her territory. Actually, she's rubbing scent glands from around her mouth and eyes in order to deposit her smell onto her territorial objects—and you just happen to be one of them.

ANCESTRAL BEHAVIORS

Like her instinctual behavior, your cat's ancestry is also a particularly potent influence. Take that spook-induced mad dash from one end of the house to the other. You know the drill: Your cat suddenly goes ballistic for no apparent reason, zipping by at the speed of light, taking corners on two legs. This behavior (which, by the way, has been clocked at 31 mph at full tilt) results from pent-up energy that suddenly overflows. Remember, your cat is a nocturnal animal and a natural hunter. The sedentary lifestyle we impose on indoor cats can literally drive them stir-crazy. The result is this nighttime frenzy.

Animal behaviorists call it "vacuum activity" and attribute it to the deprivation of opportunities to express natural, inborn urges to hunt and flee danger. Sometimes the smallest stimulus triggers this exaggerated reaction. It's really a mock attack on phantom prey. So even though there's nothing but houseflies and the occasional dirty sock to hunt in your home, and your pampered cat no longer even needs to hunt, she'll hunt anyway. It's her way of reminding you she's still got one paw in the jungle. Even Blueberry—the fetching cat I mentioned earlier—is actually playing at hunting, with her owner cast in the hapless role of repeatedly tossing paper "prey" to keep Blueberry's hunting skills as sharp as her claws.

These natural hunters with their remarkable eyesight also prefer high places to scope out the landscape for prey, or simply to rest out of reach of their own predators. For an indoor cat, the "landscape" might only be the dining room. One cat I know, housebound Jasmine, can be counted on to swing from a prized crystal chandelier the instant her owner is forgetful enough to leave the dining-room door ajar. Endowed with unmatched jumping skills, Jasmine

Jasmine insists on climbing the chandelier.

Mickey and Mouser are two cats that get along fine, except that Mickey always eats Mouser's food. Plenty of cat lovers have faced this difficult multiple-cat household problem.

leapfrogs to the door top and from there to the luxury light. To her, a chandelier's as good as a shade tree.

MULTIPLE-CAT HOUSEHOLDS

Of course, it's easier in multiple-cat broods to differentiate the wide range of cat temperaments. One of my clients has five cats. The most unflappable has taken charge; another is submissive. One has a bullying bad temper, though he also has a limitless demand for human affection and insists his owner carry him around in his arms for hours. Another prefers other cats to people.

In another multiple-cat household, Mickey and Mouser are two cats that get along fine, except that Mickey always eats Mouser's food. Their owner finally took to feeding Mouser in the bathroom and closing the door. It didn't take long for Mickey to get wise to the ploy and, in anticipation of stealing Mouser's meal, began hiding in the tub, waiting until the door was closed to leap out and consume Mouser's dinner. Their owner quickly reversed their feeding venues and kept Mickey in the bathroom instead.

Just like their king-of-the-jungle counterparts, domestic cats observe clearly defined hierarchies (though these do get periodically reshuffled). Tippy, a Maine Coon cat, is one of a household of eight. Tippy is tolerant of the rest of his roommates but rules with an iron paw. Whenever there's a dispute among the other cats, Tippy first determines exactly who started it, then ends the fracas with a whack of the paw to the perpetrator.

More commonly, the stresses of multi-cat households spark some unfortunate misbehaviors—like urinating in an owner's shoes or spraying the new sofa—all of which can remain frustratingly anonymous and difficult to pinpoint in a batch of cats.

CAT-OWNER RELATIONSHIP

Even if your cat is the solitary apple of your eye rather than only one in a bunch, all sorts of outside influences can engender quirky antics. On occasion, cats might mimic other animals. Some cats appear to imitate humans. Blinky, a silver tabby, has learned to eat steamed artichokes just the way his owner does—one leaf at a time, scraping off only the tasty pulp. Not many humans I know accomplish this as gracefully! Gizmo, a female tortoiseshell, actually has learned to share an ice cream cone, alternating licks with her owner. "Sharing" isn't an especially feline trait—among the big wild cats of Africa, only lions keep company in prides.

Alfie enjoys birdwatching.

To Gizmo, her owner is just another littermate slightly higher up the hierarchical ladder, so Gizmo naturally waits her turn dutifully instead of gobbling all the ice cream herself.

This innate deferral to another at the top of the hierarchy influences a cat's interaction with humans in other ways, too. To your cat, you're just a bigger cat, perhaps a brother, sister, or even a mother cat. Five-year-old Val will take long daily walks with his owner, staying just slightly behind, much the way kittens follow their mamas in the wild. Sometimes Val even follows his owner to work, almost doglike (though I'm sure Val's cat-loving owner would bristle at that comparison).

FELINE LEARNING

Cats don't just learn by imitation, either. They think and adapt to changing circumstances and, of course, learn by trial and error. A keen sense of smell, coupled with an unquenchable appetite, set Pepper on a nonstop mission to ferret out her own food, which her owner stored in hard-to-reach cabinets above and slightly adjacent to the top of the refrigerator. After weeks of effort, Pepper eventually figured out how to maneuver the cabinet doors open, contorting her body like an acrobat. Once Pepper learned the "trick," her otherwise childless owner had to install kid-proof locks on the cabinet doors to stop her.

The ingenuity of some of my patients doesn't always pay off as successfully as Pepper's. Alfie is an indoor city cat and enjoys sitting on the windowsill watching birds. Unfortunately, Alfie's presence on the sill would scare birds away, so they wouldn't land where Alfie could get a

Princess Kitty
A Feline Celebrity

While the overwhelming majority of cats won't perform tricks for a potato chip and wouldn't dream of working for a living, there are a few exceptions. Not too many cats I know have made it into the pages of *Newsweek* or *The Wall Street Journal*, but Princess Kitty, a professional entertainer, has. She may also be the only cat besides Morris to have her own fan club.

Princess Kitty, an ex-stray with blue-green eyes, does 75 tricks, including shaking hands, playing dead, and jumping through hoops. She even plays an impressive game of slam-dunk basketball using a miniball. Princess Kitty also plays "Happy Birthday" (to herself, of course) on a tiny piano and has mastered every obedience command, from "come" and "sit" to "stop" and "go." Don't be discouraged if your cat isn't as talented. Princess Kitty's owner happens to be a professional cat trainer.

long, yearning look at them. How did Alfie solve the problem? He developed a game of "Gotcha!"—well, almost. Alfie would sit on the floor, hiding beneath the sill to fool the birds into landing. Then he'd spring up and surprise them. Of course, the window glass thwarted Alfie's attempts to pounce, and the whole game seemed to wind up more of a surprise to the cat than the birds.

WHO'S TRAINING WHO HERE, ANYWAY?

Most cats wind up training their owners instead of the other way around. Little Guy insists on dinner on the dot, and if his owner doesn't serve it up quickly enough, Little Guy nips her on the ankle. Similarly, many cat owners tell me that while they're watching TV or reading, their cat jumps onto the couch and takes a gentle swipe at them. The typical response of most owners might include shooing the cat away, petting her, or dropping everything and following the cat around the house. Guess what? Doing those things simply trains your cat to keep taking a swipe at you.

All things considered, it's wise to avoid interpreting even "bad" behavior as negatively motivated. If a cat knocking over your prize Ming vase seems like spitefulness to you, it's more likely that your cat wants attention and wants to be chased. The minute you chase her, her behavior is reinforced and, of course, she will do it again.

Behaviorists call this "chaining" behavior. In other words, it isn't what you say to your cat, but what your cat *thinks* you say that determines her behavior. Cats are not linguists, after all. Often, what you intend and what she perceives are two entirely different things. It might help to see how your own behavior sends unintended messages to your cat.

You might, for instance, shout "Shoo!" but as long as you pay any attention, your cat interprets it as a positive response. It's like a twist on that edict to children, "Do as I say, not as I do." The connection your cat makes is: "If I stroke my owner's cheek, then she'll play with me." Thus, the cat trains you.

One of the best examples of chaining behavior I ever heard involved author Charles Dickens and his candle-snuffing cat. Dickens was penning some masterpiece by candlelight with his pet cat sitting nearby on the table. Suddenly, the candle flickered out. Dickens put down his pen, petted the cat, and relit the candle. To make a long story short, this occurred several more times until finally, Dickens realized it was the cat that was snuffing out the flame. His cat, you see, made the connection that when he snuffed out the candle, Dickens would pet him.

Many owners are unaware of how their actions inadvertently reinforce behaviors that actually teach their cats to do certain things, and some lessons cats learn can result in annoyances. One of my clients spends hours each day opening and closing doors to let her four cats in, then out, then in again. Each cat gives the owner a personal signal. One scratches the door and one even climbs the screen. Another signals her with a look, as if to say "So?" Of course, the owner always obliges. Now, her new little gray tabby kitten simply sits staring at the door handle, expecting it to open by magic. Guess what? It does!

Charles Dickens and his candle-snuffing cat.

When it comes to training their owners, some cats are downright masterful, using tactics that border on psychological warfare. For example, take King Kat (maybe the name already says it all). King Kat will only drink water from a running faucet in the sink. Once, King Kat was left with a next-door neighbor when his owner went away on a business trip. When King Kat wanted a drink, he led his cat-sitter to the sink, then immediately leaped up to sip when she turned on the faucet. When King Kat's owner came home to claim him, the cat-sitter mentioned how cute King Kat's habit was and how eagerly he jumped up for his drink. "What?" asked the stunned owner, "King Kat can't jump." Oh yes, he can—he simply prefers that his owner lift him. With his owner away, King Kat was wily enough to know he'd have to make it up there on his own.

How is it that we allow ourselves to be bamboozled by a furry being barely one-tenth our size? Frankly, it's hard not to admire cats' cleverness. King Kat obviously wanted attention and took advantage of his owner's willingness to cater to him. Yet King Kat's tactics also show that cats can reassess situations rapidly and that they're intelligent enough to solve problems.

Speaking of water, despite cats' ancestry as desert animals, they happen to be darn good swimmers. They just don't want us to know that. They figure they do a pretty good job grooming themselves without our having to bathe them. However, when each of my client's five cats inadvertently fell into her newly

King Kat will only drink from a running faucet.

installed swimming pool, they all gave new meaning to the phrase "walk on water." They were excellent swimmers—and fast.

FUN WITH FOOD

Cats may hate water, but they love food. Cats' food fetishes can be quite bizarre. One of my patients, Beethoven, adores cantaloupe and honeydew melon and will race from the other side of the house if his owner has a melon buried among the food brought from the supermarket. For some reason, Beethoven has no interest in watermelon, but Dasher does, and when chomping on watermelon, this cat even puts the seeds off to the side in a neat little pile.

Another client tells me she has to spell out the word "s-h-r-i-m-p." Otherwise, the mere mention of the word causes a stampede of six racing cats bumping over each other and over the furniture to hightail it into the kitchen. Her cats prefer the peel 'n eat kind, she says. She's so impressed with this cat antic that she even has her cats perform the stunt for company.

While another cat, M&M, doesn't watch movies, he seems to love the junk foods that go along with viewing, including popcorn, pretzels, and potato chips. This is probably because of the salt. Cats' tongues have few receptors for sweets, although another client's cat cagily chews off only the coating of chocolate-covered donuts, leaving the now-gummy cake part remaining. (Of course, chocolate isn't good for cats.) Additionally, though one red tabby I know doesn't actually eat grapes, she does love to pick them out of the fruit bowl and bat them around the house.

Most people believe that cats are solitary animals. While it's true they can get along alone just fine and are not pack animals, there is sufficient anecdotal

One of the author's clients spends hours each day letting her cats in and out—a common dilemma for many cat owners.

Cats' food fetishes can be very entertaining. Some cats will actually eat fruit, but most cats just think that grapes make *great* toys.

evidence that indicates that domesticated house cats definitely enjoy company and, if left alone for long periods without stimulation, they can languish. However, one owner may have gone overboard in his interpretation of just how much his cat missed him when he was gone on business trips. During his owner's absences, Dickey would hardly eat. Instead, he carefully and methodically placed every morsel of hard food pellets around the house, and it took the owner days to find and clean up the food. The owner concluded that this behavior meant that Dickey was angry at being left alone. While there may be a degree of truth to that, it isn't quite the whole story. What actually was going on was a behavior cats exhibit that is just like their counterparts in the wild. Dickey was burying food/prey to keep it in a safe place, away from competitors. Most importantly, not knowing when he might eat again, Dickey was conserving his food. You may notice your own cat making scraping motions around his dinner bowl, even on the floor tiles. Don't assume he doesn't like his meal—he is "burying" it and will just come back later to nibble at it again.

In fact, cats are natural nibblers, consuming between 12 and 20 small meals over the course of a day. This, together with their nocturnal lifestyle, is why you're likely to see their food untouched during the day but discover it all gone by morning. One client didn't know this and was troubled by her cat Ginger's constant habit of waking her up at four o'clock each morning. It turned out that every night, Ginger was locked in the bedroom with her owner, with kitty litter and water but no food. Naturally, when Ginger got the itch to nibble in the middle of the night, who else but her owner could open the door for her?

MORE NUTTY ANTICS

Of course, cats commonly wake their owners; it's one of the most frequently heard grievances. But sometimes there's a good reason—Molly wakes up her owner because the owner snores. In an apparent effort to thwart disturbances in her own catnaps (which, by the way, amount to about 18 hours a day—nature's way of keeping cats ever ready for hunting), Molly licks her owner's tongue to interrupt the blasted snoring.

Not all behaviors are easily explained, though. Some antics are just downright uncanny. Copernicus was always an outdoor cat that would come inside only for food and, once in a while, just to be petted by the children of the family. At all other times, Copernicus preferred being outdoors on the family's wooded property among the birds and chipmunks. But one day, one of the children became ill enough to require several weeks of bed rest. Without so much as an invitation, Copernicus surrendered his own playtime and stayed with the child constantly, stretched across the back of the sofa by day and sleeping next to her in bed at night. The moment the child was well enough to return to school, Copernicus went back to the woods.

WHY CATS LOVE A CAT-HATER

Such enigmatic behavior really may never be explained. But other conundrums do have an explanation. TeeCee, an all-white cat, always makes a beeline for the only cat-hater in the room. His owners—not to mention their cat-hating visitors—are perplexed by the behavior. To understand why, it helps to remember that cats see us simply as giant cats, and they are intimidated by the stares of other cats. TeeCee is very docile and had some serious early-life traumas, not the least of which were being tossed out of a car as a kitten and getting singed by the fire under the family furnace. It's understandable that he spends most of his time under the bed.

When and if he enters a room full of people, he's very shy. What TeeCee really sees, of course, is a room full of other cats, except that they're all larger and louder than he is. All these person-cats are staring at him, thinking how beautiful and graceful he is. This makes him very uncomfortable. Then he spies the only person-cat in the room who's not staring at him—the cat-hater. The cat-hater, meanwhile, keeps still and silently hopes TeeCee will ignore him and approach someone else. But all TeeCee knows is that he's feeling intimidated by all those person-cat stares, and he wants to seek out a safe lap. The only one in the room not moving, not waving his paw-hands, not meowing, and not staring at TeeCee is the cat-hater, the least intimidating person-cat in the room. TeeCee makes a beeline right for him.

Understanding Your Cat

One of my clients once commented to me, "I'm six feet tall and Shorty here is only six inches off the ground. So how is it that he has me wrapped around his little paw? I believe he's manipulating me." The answer seems to lie in the fact that living with cats is a lot like living with kids. They are constantly showing you more about yourself.

Pets represent different things to different people. Whether kitten or adult, the feline that chooses to make her home with us is certain to be full of surprises. They are only surprises until we bear in mind that our little companion has certain inborn instincts that have been inherited and reinforced by lessons learned at her mother's knee.

HUNTING

As a natural hunter, the youngster in a pride of lions (or a litter of kittens) brings her hard-won prize back to the den. Little Fluffy, a patient of mine, has a special hideaway, a corner of a closet, that he considers his private hangout. His family soon learns that whenever anything is missing in the house, the first place to look is Fluffy's cubbyhole. An amazing variety of loot may be stashed away—socks, bras, panties, or toys.

Shadow, a silver tabby, had started life as a street cat and had the scars to prove it. Sometimes, to her new family's consternation, Shadow would present them with a gift. A passionate mouser, she daily deposited her latest specimen at her mistress's feet, occasionally with trap attached. Another great trophy hunter was Bingo, whose greatest joy was liberating items from neighbors' yards, driveways, and sandboxes—small toys, balls, even an occasional sneaker, dragged home by the laces. Mission accomplished, Bingo would swish his tail and saunter off as if to say, "all in a day's work."

The urge to hunt has nothing to do with the urge to eat. Cat owners sometimes wonder why their well-fed pets insist on presenting them with fresh prey. Thus "honored," the owner may recoil in horror and anger, especially if the prey is half-alive and struggling. If scolded, the poor cat is totally puzzled and finds the owner's attitude incomprehensible. I advise my clients to remember that their pet is only "doing what comes naturally" and to simply praise their happy hunter and remove the victim, quietly disposing of it.

IDIOSYNCRASIES

It is often the individual idiosyncrasies that make our pets such uniquely delightful companions. Max, a sleek Siamese, keeps his family on their toes just keeping track of him. Many times the phrase "curiosity killed the cat" has come too close to reality for the peace of mind of the owners. Max's insatiable curiosity leads him to investigate every nook and cranny. He has been found inside every closet in the house and in the washer, dryer, and microwave. The family tells friends that Max is the only creature that

Princess has fun riding the vacuum cleaner.

The dryer is a popular hangout for many cats. Their owners have learned never to shut the door without checking for a sleeping kitty.

knows for sure if the light stays on when you close the refrigerator door.

Most cats are scared by loud noises, but not Princess. Whenever her mistress begins to vacuum, Princess jumps on the vacuum cleaner and rides around on top of the noisy apparatus, apparently thrilled to participate in the rug-cleaning festivities.

Bella must be a very egotistical cat, because she can look at herself in a mirror for hours at a time and never get bored. She will engage in all sorts of contortions while in front of the mirror. At times, she "attacks" the image in the mirror, going through the rituals of assaulting her prey with hissing and growling. She puts on a show worthy of an Oscar.

PLAYTIME

Some high-energy play sessions can lead to unusual behavior. Playing fetch is often a favorite activity. Just say "Where's your ball?" and Freckles will search the entire house until she finds it.

Bella attacks her image in the mirror.

Chucky peruses the newspaper on his master's shoulder.

Wadded-up balls of paper or aluminum foil are often favorite toys. Anything that moves is fair game for our little hunters. A string tied at the end of a short stick with a toy fish or bird dangled above your bundle of energy will have her jumping for joy. It's excellent exercise, too.

Occasionally, cats have special rituals when playtime is over. Blue Boy buries his toys in his litter box or immerses them in his water dish. Sandy stores his toys under the rugs in his home. Lift up a rug anytime and you'll likely find a ball, a stuffed mouse, a catnip toy, and other treasures.

Another pastime some cats enjoy is riding on their owners' shoulders. Chucky climbs on his master's shoulder as soon as he settles down with the evening paper. The cat refuses to budge, showing great interest in television and pipe smoke and even kibitzing his master's weekly poker game. Another cat jumps on his mistress's head every morning when she gets out of the shower and rides around on the towel for long periods of time.

Inky lets his family know he's in the mood for fun and games by adopting a "Halloween cat" pose, arching his back and walking stiff-legged, tail erect and fur bristling as he prances enticingly.

The first day Barbara brought Giggles home, she noticed the kitten was doing

Your Health

Not only can a healthy, happy cat become an unconditional friend, companion, and pal to her adopted person, she may be beneficial to her owner's health. The act of petting a warm body and soaking up the vibrations from the purring engine within has a calming effect and can actually lower blood pressure. Mental patients have been known to improve greatly when they are allowed the company of pet cats. Increasingly, nursing homes, hospitals, juvenile detention centers, and even prisons are discovering the tranquilizing influence of physical contact with a cat.

If laughter is the best medicine, as is often said, then our feline friends deserve some sort of degree in preventive medicine. Though we may not understand why they do what they do, we get many a chuckle out of their antics.

Like Charlie, many cats love to compose contemporary music on the piano. Closing the keyboard is the only way to prevent impromptu predawn concerts.

something unusual. Giggles would put her forehead on the floor and do a lopsided somersault. Amused, Barbara would say "Alley-oop!" and cuddle the kitten every time she did it. Now, when Giggles is in a playful mood, her mistress says "Alley-oop," and Giggles will do her funny somersault.

Cats and Music

From the beginning, Charlie loved to sleep on top of the new piano. Soon he discovered the delights of the keyboard. At first, surprised by the sounds emanating from the ivories as he hopped down from his perch, he cautiously investigated. What a delightful cacophony he could create by walking on the keys! Charlie was so pleased with his new toy that the family had to be sure the keyboard was closed at night so that they wouldn't be kept awake by Charlie's nocturnal serenades.

"Music hath charms to soothe the savage beast," so the saying goes. Not always. Whenever Carl practiced his clarinet, his Siamese cat, Sheba, would go crazy, running in circles and howling so loudly she drowned out Carl's musical efforts.

Two-year-old Daisy seems to like piano music. Each evening when her mistress plays, Daisy gives her own performance. Holding her tail straight in the air, she rhythmically shifts her weight from one side to the other, lifting her legs higher and higher each time. Daisy's family calls her "Waltzing Matilda" and sings the Australian anthem to her. Daisy dances and meows right along.

Sometimes accompanying music isn't even required. Since kittenhood, Tootsie had her own vaudeville act. She frequently stood on her hind legs, waving her paws in front of her face and chest for several minutes at a time. Whether a hula or a belly dance, it was an amusing show.

INDOOR CATS

There is no question that an indoor cat lives a safer, healthier life than one that is allowed to roam. Some of my clients feel it is unkind to deprive a cat of her freedom to explore the world. Certainly, an outside cat will never be bothered by the boredom that leads to misbehavior. However, with her amazing adaptability, a feline is capable of creating a satisfying life for herself despite man's terrible invention: the door. Nevertheless, some cats are ingenious and have learned to turn doorknobs and open closed doors. The only defense against such talented creatures is to lock the door.

Twinkle was an inside cat. Her family made every effort to provide her with diversions—lots of attention, petting, games, etc. Despite all their efforts, Twinkle seemed bored out of her skull. She developed the habit of bolting through the living room door into the next room and back again. Back and forth Twinkle would go, until her mistress thought a furrow would appear in the carpet. When Twinkle came in for a regular visit, her mistress mentioned this compulsive behavior to me. I recognized the pacing as a physical release of excess energy and suggested a companion cat. Now Twinkle has a playmate to romp with and to cuddle with during quiet times. No more empty time on her paws.

Sambo declared war on his owner's boyfriend.

UNHAPPY CATS

Cats often find unique ways to signal their delight or distress to their special person. Sambo's mistress never realized that her little friend was trying to communicate with her. Sambo enlightened her in an all-too-graphic way. Sambo's mistress had a new boyfriend. This guy was persona non grata in Sambo's book. For the first week or two of the intrusion of this shady character into his home, Sambo simply glared at him, tail bristling. Gradually, Sambo further demonstrated his sense of revulsion with sneak attacks on the victim's ankles. The boyfriend didn't seem to get the message until Sambo piddled in his shoe. After a torrent of obscene words, with one shoe on and one shoe off, Mr. Boyfriend fled the apartment. After Sambo and his mistress calmed down, she realized that Sambo had sized up her male companion and understood him in ways she was too blind to see. Sambo knew best. He tried to warn her in the only way available to him: body language. (I believe Sambo had another motive too—jealousy.)

Personalities vary in cats as much as they do in people. The owner of a sister-brother pair of felines told me it was like living with Dr. Jekyll and Mr. Hyde. These two cats' characters were as different as night and day. It was sister Whitey who was the tough guy. If she'd been human, she would have worn a black leather jacket and zoomed around on a fast, noisy Harley. Whitey was definitely Boss Cat. She would stare anyone or anything down. On the other hand, Blackie was quick to retreat behind a sofa and lie low until the coast was clear. Where gentle Blackie seemed content to give affection and purr at the slightest cuddle and stroke, Whitey always would be first in line for food or prime choice of lap space. When she glared at Blackie, her eyes seemed to be saying, "Buzz off, I'm the boss here."

One cat, on seeing the carrier brought up from the basement, and sensing a trip to the vet's office, will disappear, sometimes for days, until she perceives the danger is past. The Clint Eastwood type, male or female, when placed on the examining table, will stand tall and look the veterinarian in the eye as if to say, "OK, Doc, here I am. Make my day."

There is a situation I call "kick-the-cat" syndrome. One of my clients did nothing but badmouth his cat, "There's enough cat hair around here to weave a new cat! Stink, stink, stink! I'm ready to throw in the pooper scooper and call it quits!" This fellow had a lot of personal problems—his boss, his wife, even the IRS making threatening noises at him. I felt sorry for him, but pitied his cat, PeeWee, even more. PeeWee was actually an intelligent, perceptive animal, maybe too much for her own good. Cats, like people, need to have their egos stroked and their self-esteem reinforced to bring out the warmth and love hidden in their hearts.

In exchange for a little affection, a cat will be happy to share your life. A cat doesn't care whether you're rich or poor, fat or thin, beautiful or plain. For the small expenditure of caring, nurturing, and stroking, you have a devoted companion to warm your feet on winter nights and lift your soul when you are feeling down.

Best bargain in town!

ABNORMAL BEHAVIOR

It is the consensus of the experts that the tensions of our modern-day civilization have a deteriorating effect on our pets. A recent survey indicates that there are behavioral problems in 10 to 20 percent of the cats in our midst. We have changed their behavior patterns so much from their wild state that it is small wonder that their difficulties are increasing rapidly. Also, it appears from research that a direct relationship exists between the behavior problems of the cats and those of their owners, suggesting that animals may reflect the emotional atmosphere of the household in which they live. A tense, stressful family life can adversely affect a cat's behavior, especially when owners are fearful, anxious, extremely noisy, excessively permissive, bored, or overly introverted.

If a kitten is reared in an unsuitable environment, perhaps in seclusion, or experienced a bad relationship with her mother or her human family, she may be expected to grow up to be unhappy, nervous, and timid. If she's under four months of age, she can easily be taught to deal with crises. The older she is, the more difficult it will be and the slower her response to treatment.

Although there are many cats past the point of remedial help, there are many more with innate or learned objectionable behavior patterns for which a good deal can be done. You can tell if your cat has a problem and needs help if she shows any of the following symptoms: spending the majority of her time hiding, chasing her tail, licking herself excessively, lying immobile, or constantly moving, fighting, and chasing or being chased.

Unfortunately, some owners of cats with behavior problems tolerate them

Signs of a Problem Cat

- Depression or excitability
- Loss of appetite or overeating
- Unprovoked attacks on owner or other animals
- Self-mutilation
- Hysteria
- Phobias
- Excessive crying or meowing

and do not attempt to correct their pets. However, eventually, because of embarrassment and frustration, these people look for professional help from their veterinarian or animal behaviorist.

If your cat's behavior has you at your wit's end, you can survive the ordeal if you understand what you've done to cause the problem. A lack of understanding on the owner's part can sometimes predispose a cat to misbehavior. People sometimes expect a cat to learn something that the pet cannot comprehend—she doesn't know what you expect of her.

The Effects of Inherited Nervousness

Although most cases of nervousness are basically due to environmental factors, some cats do inherit the tendency to be nervous. If a nervous cat was bred from non-nervous parents, then it is fairly certain that the nervousness is environmental. Inherited nervousness should be eliminated from the strain by not allowing such cats to breed; they should be spayed or neutered. Behavioral abnormalities that should be watched for before allowing an animal to breed are excessive timidity and fear of strangers; refusal to leave a familiar environment; sound, touch, and sight shyness; biting out of fear; excessive scratching; fear of sudden changes; and excessive activity. Any of these traits would most likely be inherited by the offspring and compounded by exposure to the nervous queen. The vast majority of offspring of the shy, fear-biting, and scratching queen will be neurotic, even though the studs may be normal and friendly creatures. In addition to the direct inheritance of shyness, the behavior of the mother is likely to influence the kittens to react violently to strangers and other disturbing influences. This shyness is not overcome by training.

The Effects of Physical Disorders

When I examine a cat that is brought to me because of abnormal behavior, there are many factors that I consider. We must always investigate the possibility of a physical disorder as a cause of any abnormal behavior before we say that the cat has a mental problem. I usually give the animal a complete physical checkup, looking for one of the disorders that can affect behavior, including worms, thyroid ailments, spinal disk disorder, poisoning, constipation, diarrhea, dental problems, urinary ailments, allergic reactions, milk fever in a nursing queen, sex organ malfunction, and anal gland infection. Diseases such as rabies, meningitis, distemper, and epilepsy also could be causes. Brain tumors, abscesses, ear mites, and such traumatic events as a blow to the head or an inner-ear infection can cause abnormal behavior and affect a cat's temperament. I have seen cats with head injuries undergo loss of social and sexual drives, show complete lethargy, and regress to kitten habits—or even further back to the point of primitive, wild feline behavior.

You should be aware that any changes in the normal behavior of your cat could indicate that something is wrong. When a cat is sick, she often becomes hostile to the people she loves. She can even become angry and act like a wild animal. However, we have to confess that we ourselves have a tendency to act the same way when we have a headache, a fever, or a gnawing pain.

A complete physical checkup is in order to investigate the possibility of a physical disorder as a cause of any abnormal behavior.

Cats seem to have a low threshold for pain and high sensitivity to discomfort or illness. That is why your cat will sometimes run away from you and hide when she is not feeling well. The cat is scared and wishes to be left alone. In the wild, cats either get well or die. Fortunately, an alert cat owner can seek professional help and should do so as quickly as possible. After elimination of the organic problem, the abnormal behavior generally clears up.

The Effects of Drugs and Alcohol

Prolonged use or an overdose of tranquilizers or sedatives can change behavior. Some drugs accumulate in the bloodstream and gradually, over a period of time, cause dysfunction in mental abilities. If the cat becomes sleepy or groggy under a particular medication, have your veterinarian check it out to be sure there are no sedatives in it that are affecting the cat's mental ability. Cats that behave oddly have also been found to be under the influence of marijuana.

A cat behaving abnormally can conceivably be under the influence of alcohol, especially around Christmastime, when at least one pet is always brought to me that has consumed too much eggnog. You can tell when a cat is hung over—the eyes are bleary and she is listless, with manifestations of a headache. At a recent veterinary convention, there was a discussion about the increase in the number of alcoholic cats. Unfortunately, chronic drinking generally starts as a gag at a party. The feline victim acquires a taste for the stuff and becomes a sneaky party drinker.

Too much catnip can cause many behavioral changes. Catnip should only be given occasionally, not as an everyday treat.

The Effects of Catnip

Most cats, but not all, respond to catnip and its mild aphrodisiac qualities, and it can be used as a positive reinforcer in the retraining of problem cats. Bribery does work well in influencing a cat's good behavior.

However, excessive amounts of catnip can cause hyperactivity in a cat. Some owners give their pet all the catnip that the animal wants, and this can lead to many behavioral changes. Some cats become hooked on the plant and behave in strange ways. Catnip should only be given as an occasional pick-me-up and not as an everyday treat. Cats exposed to catnip-filled toys sniff, lick, chew, roll over, rub their cheeks, scratch, and sometimes salivate.

Cats that have consumed too much catnip over a long period of time become glassy-eyed, staring into space and crying and meowing a great deal (as when they are in heat). They tread ground with their paws and will engage in sexual activity with their catnip toys.

The Effects of Aging

As senility affects the various organs of the body, so will there be a gradual change in some behavioral patterns in the aging cat. As she gets older, the cat seems to change her attitude toward her human family, perhaps wanting more and more to be left alone in comfort instead of romping and playing. The cat may sometimes seem to be a little irritable and not want to be handled. Accede to these simple demands and try to be more sympathetic, loving, and patient.

Older cats may become irritable and easily upset by change. This is especially true if they have health problems like this cat, which is blind in one eye.

The behavior of old cats is very similar to that of elderly people. They should get extra special considerations, such as more attention and more petting when they are in the mood for it. Old cats may meow and make other noises at night for reassurance from their owners. They become more insecure with age and require more cuddling and loving at times. The older they are, the more dependent on you they become.

Cats quickly become fixed in their habits and are easily upset by change. In their old age especially, they need a daily routine, and any deviation may annoy them. They might become irritable and hiss occasionally. Be patient with these old folks and remember the days when they did everything to please you.

As old age creeps up on your cat, you will notice diminishing vigor in every activity. There may also be some inconveniences to you and your family, such as a wet spot on the rug once in a while and the need to prepare special diets, but such things are a small price to pay for all the years of love and loyalty.

The Effects of Loneliness

Misbehavior stemming from loneliness is varied and can assume neurotic proportions. Today, it is more the rule than the exception that owners vacate the premises several hours each day, leaving pets to entertain themselves.

Although most cats adjust magnificently to being left alone, there are some who would rather have companionship, and the resultant loneliness and boredom can cause abnormal behavior. Some lonely cats will groom themselves excessively, which can lead to fur-pulling and self-mutilation; others will literally chew their tails to shreds.

Some cats who do not like seclusion will cry incessantly.

I met one cat in particular that was different from most cats. Mimi never felt secure when she was left alone. She always wanted human companionship, and other animals would not do. When Mimi was left alone in the house, even for a brief time, she got extremely

Mimi can't tolerate being left alone at night.

nervous, becoming destructive by tearing at curtains, furniture, or anything else that got in her way. When her owners tried to keep her out of the bedroom at night, Mimi had an anxiety attack and clawed on the door. As a result, Mimi is allowed in the bedroom and sleeps with her head on the pillow next to the husband and wife.

Some people who leave their cats alone for long periods salve their conscience by leaving the television set running for the entertainment of their pet. However, a group of animal psychologists in Germany that has studied the effects of television on pets has found that too much TV can make animals neurotic. It appears that if a cat watches too much TV, she becomes nervous and can suffer acute loss of appetite. However, a small amount of TV will not hurt the average cat. If a radio is left on quietly, the low voices

While too much television can be detrimental to cats, a small daily dose can entertain a lonely feline. Videotapes of the owner or commercially available videos designed especially for cats are both good suggestions.

A fish tank is another way to distract bored and lonely cats. Some cats are captivated for hours by watching the fish swim around.

and music tend to be soothing to a cat. Some people make sound recordings of their voices and play them quietly all day for the lonely cat. This seems to satisfy the insecure cat by reassuring her that her owner is nearby. This works well with misbehaving cats that get into all kinds of mischief because of boredom.

If you cannot get another kitten or puppy to keep the cat company, see to it that your cat has lots of toys and a perch on a window with a view. Another object that holds a cat's attention is a fish tank—the "kitty TV." Watching fish swim around fascinates some cats.

The Effects of Anthropomorphism (Humanizing)

Many owners treat their cats as if they were humans. Sometimes humanizing is harmful to the cat because it goes against their normal physical and psychological behavior.

One couple treats their cat as a surrogate child, dressing him in infant clothing, talking to him in baby talk, and allowing him to eat at the dinner table with them. On Halloween night, with all of them in full costume, they go trick-or-treating, much to the anguish and fright of the cat.

Another woman insists on her cat taking a shower with her every morning. Although most cats dislike bathing intensely, Kit Kat has gotten used to it and come to

People who treat their cats as surrogate children may be going against the normal physical and psychological behavior of the pets. What is good for a human isn't always good for a pet.

really enjoy it. However, the excessive soaping caused dry, itchy skin. What is good for a human isn't always good for a pet.

There are some people who would rather be in the company of their cats than with other people. They are introverted because of disappointment or disillusionment in the human race and turn to their cats instead. There is one woman who has 10 to 15 cats living with her, all sleeping together on their king-sized bed and eating at the dining room table at the same time. She claims that cats are more honest than people and never lie to you. She says that when your human friends won't talk to you, your cats always will. She often quotes Ernest Hemingway, who said, "A cat has absolute honesty. Male or female, a cat will show you how it feels about you. People hide their feelings for various reasons, but cats never do."

"When your human friends won't talk to you, your cats always will".

69

Antisocial Cats

Some cats have antisocial tendencies and will not associate with other cats or people. Introverted cats may stay close to their human family and will have nothing to do with strangers. Aggressive cats may lash out at a moment's notice. Sometimes this disdain is merely feigned, and sometimes it is real—it depends on the cat's mood at the time. When truly antisocial behavior is ingrained in a cat, it may be impossible to cure. However, many cats recover well enough to coexist with their peers and with people.

Shyness and Timidity

Shyness is usually inherited, but can also be acquired by a kitten that is nursed by a timid queen. In cases where the shyness is inherited, it is doubtful that the cat can ever be converted into an extrovert. Lots of time, love, and patience is needed to accustom these cats to people.

When a timid queen has kittens, it is best to remove these kittens as soon as they can eat by themselves at around four weeks of age so that the mother doesn't impart her own distrustful personality to her offspring. If the kittens stay longer than four weeks, they will learn to act as she does—unfriendly and fearful of the world around them. Kittens can also develop shyness if they have no contact with humans by the time they are 12 weeks old. By this time, they will have developed an extreme fear of people.

Shy cats are usually submissive in nature, lacking confidence in themselves and in the human race. They panic easily and will bite or scratch when cornered. A shy and frightened cat will confront you in a sideways stance with an arched back and a lowered crouch. She is as scared of you as you are of her. A skittish cat exhibits a crouching gait, a tail carried low, dilated pupils, and slow, deliberate movements until she gets into a hiding place where she feels secure. Some scared cats will even burrow under bedclothes to hide from people. Extremely wary cats seek dark corners or closets and spend most of their time in these safe spots, leaving the area for food at night. A litter box should be available nearby, or house-soiling accidents will occur.

Because of emotional instability and lack of belief in her own abilities, a shy cat must be handled gently. Never approach her too quickly or make a sudden movement toward her. Kneel down and talk to her quietly, petting her under the chin and rubbing

Some skittish cats will literally cling to their owners, fearful of a separation from the one person in the world they trust.

her ears to reassure her.

Be slow and quiet in all your dealings with an anxious cat. If a shy cat is pushed too hard, she may strike at you in annoyance.

Timid cats do not like to be held and are not relaxed in the company of people. They are reserved with everyone except their owner, to whom they become acclimated over a period of time. Some skittish cats, suffering from overdependence, will literally cling to their owners, fearful of a separation from the one person in the world they trust. They are not playful and fear all kinds of noises.

If a fearful kitten was intimidated by her mother or siblings between 4 and 12 weeks of age (the socialization period), she may be easily frightened by other cats or animals for the rest of her life. Sometimes the runt of the litter develops into a timid cat because she is neglected by her mother and littermates. A cat becomes a shy adult unless an observant owner notices this deprivation and gives the outcast extra handling and petting.

If there is a shy cat among a group of cats, very often the social outcast will be attacked by the other cats in the group. These castaways become wary of the other cats and will growl and crouch when they are approached. It is best for a timid cat to be in a household by herself with no other pets around. Such cats want and need all the attention for themselves in order to build up their confidence.

People should always act happy and very friendly when they are with a reserved cat. This kind of pet is extremely sensitive to her owner's moods. If a person is in a bad mood, he or she should stay away from the timid cat.

Timid cats will progressively get worse with age if they are left untreated. Patience and loving care are the prime ingredients of the cure. The older the cat, the longer it will take to cure, but generally a great deal of progress can be made in two to three weeks.

Abnormal Cats

Tranquilizers (or hormones for shy, cowardly male cats) and a gradual exposure to people and noises will help most timid cats, but it is a long and slow process to instill trust in the mind of a distrustful animal. To desensitize a shy cat to all the normal noises of a household, provide a large cage in a quiet corner where a wary cat can feel safe and secure while listening to all the noises. In time, move the cage into the living room or other busy room. Gradually begin to leave the cage door open so that the cat can come out of her own accord when she feels more secure.

One of the best therapies for an introverted, shy, and lonely cat is playtime with her owner. The more the owner plays with her, the closer the bond between owner and cat. Play is much more efficient than any tranquilizer in normalizing your cat's temperament. It is best to play with the cat when there is no one else around. She will be more relaxed and uninhibited in a one-on-one setting.

In socializing a shy kitten or adult cat, gently touch her all over, picking her up and hugging her while whispering words of endearment. After a while, allow some friends to do the same, showing the cat plenty of affection in words and touch. Do not force anyone on these shy individuals too quickly. Let them make up their own minds when the time is right to be held by a stranger. Kittens will usually respond much more quickly than an adult cat.

Overdependency

Some shy and timid cats form a mother fixation with their owner and are constantly at his or her side. Any separation can cause extreme anxiety, with consequential misbehavior. The cat acts and thinks like a kitten when she's around her "mother." When the affection is reciprocated, she will purr and knead, often sucking on some part of the owner's anatomy such as the neck, ear lobe, fingers, or arms. To overcome this dependency, other members of the family should be involved in caring for and playing with the cat. Sucking on the owner should also be discouraged. It is advisable to get the cat interested in other activities, such as playing with toys and going for walks outdoors on a leash. Anything that represses these infantile behaviors is worth trying. To prevent overdependency, it is important for the kitten to be handled by several different people during her early weeks so that she gets accustomed to more than one person. If a kitten only has contact with one person in her early introduction to people, she might attach herself emotionally to that person and become insecure around any other individual.

Aggression

An anxious, fretting cat can easily become aroused and react aggressively. All cats react differently to stress. Some fight, others run away, and some will attack anyone or anything in the vicinity, even though that person or animal is not the source of the anxiety. Some highly emotional cats become excited by too much rough play with people or other animals and may overreact by biting and scratching.

Close to 20 percent of owners who own aggressive cats believe that abuse from their pets is a normal part of cat ownership, and so it would seem reasonable to assume that a very large number of cat owners are being scratched and bitten daily. They do little or nothing to prevent this behavior, for several reasons. The most important of

An anxious, fretting cat can easily become aroused and react aggressively.

these reasons is the fallacious idea that aggressive behavior is normal. If owners believe that a cat's natural behavior includes biting and scratching them occasionally, then it follows that they also believe that they can do relatively little to prevent it. Consequently, these owners would not seek help for their cat's misbehavior because they do not consider the pet to be misbehaving.

Another important reason for the indifference toward aggressive behavior in cats is the fact that a bite or scratch from a cat is not usually severe, and the victim ordinarily does not have to rush to the hospital emergency room. However, a hospital trip is often necessary following an equally aggressive act on the part of a dog. In general, pet dogs are bigger than pet cats, their bites inflict larger wounds, and the owners are subject to lawsuits. Who ever heard of a cat biting the mailman or tearing the seat off the pants of the trash collector?

This leads to two further reasons why aggressive behavior in cats is perceived as less noteworthy than similar behavior in dogs. One is the place of occurrence and the other is the object of the aggression. It is rare to hear of cats attacking anyone outside the confines of their own homes. Hostile displays, therefore, are usually directed toward owners, relatives, or friends of the family. Under these circumstances, the cat owner maintains a rather comfortable sense of security. The incident has not been observed by outsiders, and therefore no hostile witnesses can be brought into play in a legal action. Besides, what "friend" would initiate a suit? The owners simply treat the injury, apologize, and comment that "cats will be cats."

Some cat owners do attempt to deal with aggressive behaviors in their animals, even though they still believe that the behavior is normal and will occur if they do not act in a certain manner. These owners avoid direct physical contact with the animal, either by ignoring it indoors or by relegating it to the outside world, permitting entry only at mealtime, after dark, or during a storm. This arrangement not only serves as an effective barrier to aggression but also provides further support for the belief that cats are aloof creatures. Indeed, cats will obligingly withdraw under these conditions, living in virtual independence of the humans in the household. Dealing with aggressiveness in this manner is hardly ideal and renders the term "pet" inappropriate.

Some of my clients, despite being witnesses to and recipients of unprovoked attacks by the family cat, quietly deny that actual aggression is taking place. More often than not, these owners will not even discuss the issue. When a friend is bitten, the owner makes little acknowledgment of the act, and absolutely no disciplinary measures are taken. Quite often the owner fails to utter even a verbal reprimand.

We see the same personality types in dog owners who seem to take a kind of sadistic delight in the fact that they own an animal that has a dozen or more bites to his credit. Such owners, regardless of whether their animal is a dog or cat, may be venting their own hostility or anger through the actions of the animal. However, dealing with deep-seated emotional problems of the owner is not within the realm of this book. The purpose of this book is to assist the majority of people who seek professional help for their problem pets—well-adjusted human beings who simply have little knowledge of animal behavior.

In most cases, by the time cat owners admit that they have an aggressive pet and are prepared to treat the behavior as a correctable problem, the situation has reached an intolerable level. The hostile patients, as a rule, are older cats who have bitten or scratched once too often. In desperation, and generally as a last resort, the owners decide it is time to seek professional help. I find that many of these animals have a long combat history. Nothing had been done to prevent the nipping in kittenhood, and the behavior had increased in frequency and intensity. The kitten grew stronger, and the nips became vicious bites. Since the owner had set no limits on the type of play permitted, the cat had established its own rules. These cat owners have to be guided through training procedures involving protective clothing and gentle interaction with their pet. Success is usually achieved, and the happy owners realize that you can teach an old cat new tricks.

Many aggressive cats behave the way they do because they had little or no contact with humans when they were kittens. They might learn to trust their owners but are wary of strangers and may react violently toward them. If a cat becomes too aggressive to her owner, one remedy for the situation is to keep the cat in a dark room and leave her in solitary confinement, visiting her only when you bring her food twice a day. The theory is that she will look forward to your visits and become more docile toward you. At the beginning, the visits should be brief, but gradually more and more time should be spent with the cat, talking to her and petting her so that you can eventually conquer her insecurity.

Other causes of aggression are boredom and loneliness. Without anyone or anything to play with, the cat will resort to attacking ankles, which make tempting moving targets. The cat may also enjoy jumping on newspapers while you are reading. Belligerence in a cat may also be the result of being ignored by her owner. When a cat misses her formerly regular play sessions, the cat becomes resentful and may start attacking members of the family for attention. Other cats become hostile when they are confined to quarters and not allowed to roam freely outdoors as they once did. These claustrophobic cats also show their displeasure by urinating and defecating in the house.

Some aggressive cats are just playing, while others are seeking attention, resisting restraint, or asking you to stop whatever you're doing. Acts of aggression are sometimes taught inadvertently by owners who play rough games with their kittens. This encourages the cat to grab and bite their fingers and teaches her that it's all right to be aggressive.

Foreign odors on companion cats cause them to fight, because each doesn't recognize the other's odor. For example, when one of them returns from the veterinary hospital with strange odors on her, a fight will ensue. Another common time for a fight is after the cats have a bath. A remedy for this situation is to rub each cat separately with a clean towel before the bath and then rub each cat with her own towel after the bath. As for the cat returning from the veterinary hospital, it is advisable to wipe the cat off with a towel before returning home.

The fact that there are a variety of causes for aggressive cats serves to emphasize a very important point: There are no general methods for handling aggression. Techniques for inducing or restoring acceptable pet behavior, regardless of the misbehavior, are very much dependent upon the combined factors of inheritance and experiences in the social and physical environments. Certain principles of animal behavior have been formulated from studies conducted by scientists researching instinct, temperament, and learning, but there is no universal strategy for dealing with the various forms of misbehavior. This is particularly true in cases of aggression. What follows is a discussion of the various causes and types of aggression and some techniques to use when you are faced with each problem.

SIGNS OF AN AGGRESSIVE CAT

A shy and frightened cat will confront you in a sideways stance with an arched back and a lowered crouch. However, if she is turned directly facing you with an arched back, she is ready to attack. Usually, she will also hiss or bare her teeth. A cat that arches her back with an elevated rear end and that is in a slightly crouched position is ready to fight. You should handle a cat carefully if she is lying on her back looking up at you. This is a normal position that cats assume when defending themselves. The cat might be daring you to scratch her stomach. She might be very content and want affection, but if she is in a bad mood, she could attack you when you touch her. Try to figure out her intentions before you rub her belly. Avoid actions that may be misinterpreted as hostile, such as petting her rump or tickling her belly.

Other signs that indicate that a cat is about to strike at someone or something are a lashing tail, dilated pupils in her eyes, a crouched position with laid-back, flat ears, and rolling over just before she strikes. When confronting a nervous cat, avoid staring directly into her eyes. An aggressive cat might take this gesture as a challenge to her security. Look either below her eyes or to one side as you approach this type of cat.

A shy and frightened cat will confront you in a sideways stance with an arched back.

In trying to make friends with an antagonistic cat, do not force yourself on her too quickly. You must learn to recognize the cat's limit to the amount of petting she will accept from you. Do not lift up an aggressive cat and put her in your lap in order to pet her. She might resent it. Pet her in her own desired spot, such as on a chair or a sofa.

FITS OF RAGE—MENTAL LAPSES

Some male cats suddenly and inexplicably bite their owners while apparently enjoying being petted. Some theorize that this act of violence during a pleasurable experience is similar to the biting of the female's neck by the tomcat during copulation. If this act of biting becomes persistent, neutering and/or hormones can provide relief.

There are other cats, both male and female, that without apparent provocation explode into a growling, spitting rage. The slightest external stimulation elicits a well-directed attack. Verbal and physical attempts to interrupt the aggression are to no avail, and so abrupt and violent is the behavior that observers generally—and wisely—retreat. The brave individual who remains is in danger of being severely injured. The fury stops as suddenly as it begins, and the cat reverts to its typical, affectionate behavior. However, directly following the fit of rage, the cat does not recognize familiar faces and appears dazed, with a distant look in her eyes. Afterward, she appears subdued and shaken.

There are no known causes for this bizarre behavior, but in recent years, a brain malfunction has been blamed for this sudden aggression. There is no current successful treatment for this behavioral problem. Some cats have been helped with

A cat that is about to strike will hiss or bare her teeth, lash her tail, and face her enemy head-on.

anticonvulsant drugs, similar to the ones used in treating epilepsy. The reasoning behind this treatment is that the unprovoked attacks are believed to be a type of seizure. Lifelong administration of tranquilizers can offer some relief.

Other causes of rage in cats can be reaction to some kind of pain, territorial disputes, courting behavior, competition for food, fear of a traumatic event, or personality clashes with the owner.

Some cats react violently because they have had enough petting and want to be left alone. Experts believe that continuous pleasurable stimulation can overexcite a sensitive cat, causing aggressive behavior.

There is a normal courting behavior that sometimes results in a human getting bitten. Its cause is a courting instinct in female cats in which they try to bite the object of their affection immediately after orgasm. In other encounters of a nonsexual nature, the cat sometimes gets so excited by affectionate behavior that she suddenly bites. An example of this is when a normally affectionate altered female cat jumps on an owner's bed, crawls up by the person's neck while purring loudly, kneads, and then suddenly, after a few minutes, bites the owner's neck. This behavior is easily avoided. As soon as the cat begins purring and kneading you, push her away or move away from her.

AGGRESSIVE BEHAVIOR TOWARD OTHER ANIMALS

Occasionally, clients come to me with a cat that acts aggressively toward other family pets. In most cases, the fighting is a form of dominance testing, either because a new animal has been brought into the cat's territory or because kittens have grown up and one tries to show the others who's boss. In some ways, animals are more civilized than man. Seldom does one animal assume dominance over another by killing. Instead, ritualistic display behaviors successfully establish one member as leader and place the others in a descending order of submission.

If one cat is a bully and picks fights with other animals, placing a bell on her collar will help reduce sneak attacks. For a timid cat, mood elevators and hormones may help instill more courage.

CAT VS. CAT

When two cats are fighting for leadership, both cats may spit, snarl, assume threatening postures, and perhaps engage in sparring, but eventually, and most often without any fur flying, one of the cats submits and quietly withdraws. This testing may take place many times until leadership is determined, then recur occasionally during succeeding weeks and months whenever the submissive member decides to take another crack at leadership. It is quite normal behavior, and unless the owner sees that the fighting is becoming physically harmful to one of the animals, it is best to let the cats work it out for themselves. They are much better equipped to establish their places in the household than the owners are.

When introducing two aggressive cats into a household, you can use Valium or a similar tranquilizer prescribed by a vet to slow them down until they get used to one another. Giving hormones to both of them will also help slow the aggression. Feed

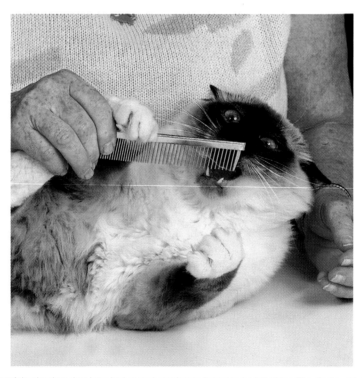

Some cats react violently when they have had enough petting and want to be left alone. The alert owner can usually tell when this is about to happen by noting the cat's increasingly annoyed body language.

each cat separately, very far apart at first, and gradually lessen the distance. It may take several weeks, but eventually they will tolerate each other from a distance. Keep moving the dishes closer until they tolerate each other while eating side by side. Eventually, a truce will be declared and they will be able to live in the house together even if they still don't like each other. If one of the fighting cats is a tomcat, neutering will slow him down 80 to 90 percent of the time. Treatment for severe cases of aggression requires the supervision of a veterinarian or an animal psychologist who is trained in these matters.

Misdirected Aggression

Some normal cats suddenly turn into psychotic raging beasts after seeing or sniffing a strange or rival cat. They will attack anything or anyone in the vicinity, not necessarily the cat that provoked the stressful encounter. Many an owner has been a victim as a result. Be sure to remember that agitated cats always have dilated pupils and wag their tails. Be wary of cats that are in a tense emotional state. They will attack if provoked any further. While a cat is feeling hostile, it is best to wait at a safe distance until the cat calms down, speaking to her in a calm and soft tone. If two cats are actually fighting, do not attempt to separate them. Yell at them or spray them with water to surprise them into stopping. In a group of cats, there is usually one troublemaker that starts fighting with anyone that is near her when she is startled by a loud noise, the presence of a strange person, or an alien odor on one of the cats.

It is quite normal for hissing, posturing, and sparring to occur when two cats are vying for leadership in the household. Usually, this behavior will subside with time.

Despite the myth that dogs and cats are natural enemies, a kitten or tolerant cat can be great company for a lonely dog.

Fighting Like Cats and Dogs

I never cease to be amazed at the number of people who still believe the myth that cats and dogs are natural enemies and that peaceful coexistence is not possible. Not only is it possible for a cat to tolerate a dog, but it is more the rule than the exception that the two can become marvelous companions. I often have clients who come to me with misbehaving dogs. After carefully taking a history, I may find that the dog's misbehavior stems from loneliness. In these cases, I suggest that the clients obtain a companion for their pet. Unless circumstances are completely prohibitive, I strongly recommend a kitten as the new addition.

Many clients initially resist my suggestion and tell me that their dog would never get along with a cat. I often discover, however, that the real reason for their resistance is lack of knowledge about cats. When these owners do follow through, the results can appear to be miraculous; not only does the dog's misbehavior stop, but the two animals become intimate playmates and the owners discover the fun of raising their first kitten.

However, if you have a misbehaving dog, please don't rush out into the night to purchase a kitten with the idea that this will be a panacea for your problems. It is wise to remember that there are some dogs that consider all cats to be prey and that there are cats that will attack any dog on sight. I would particularly caution people who have never owned a cat. Before anyone obtains a kitten, or any other animal for that matter, he should get explicit instructions on proper rearing. Without thorough investigation, it is impossible to determine the source of any particular pet problem, and introducing a new kitten could present more problems than you had at the start. For one thing, you could end up with a dead kitten. Although it takes a relatively short time for a kitten to learn to defend herself effectively, gradual, protected introduction is the rule.

It is comparatively easy to bring a new kitten into a dog's domain, but it may be quite different to bring a new puppy into a grown cat's domain. It is, of course, possible to teach a cat to accept a new dog, but it will generally take a longer period of time. The young puppy has few defenses that are effective against a cat whose home has been invaded.

Before introducing a new dog into a household with cats, it is advisable to play recordings of dogs barking in order to get the cats used to it. You can desensitize the cats to the barking by playing it at a low volume at first and then gradually increasing the noise level. You have to introduce a cat and dog slowly, at their own pace, until both are comfortable with each other.

I am reminded of a very amusing story about a brave cat in a multi-dog family:

Sambo is a black cat, part Siamese, who took a lot of punishment from four dogs in the household. They chased him and teased him whenever and wherever they could. Finally, after years of being pushed around, Sambo made his stand. When cornered one day by all four barking dogs, Sambo let one of them have it right on the nose with claws fully unsheathed. The yelling dog frightened the others and they all ran away, leaving Sambo to reign as king of the house forever after. Sambo had decided that enough was enough. He was now chairman of the board.

NIPPING NIPPING IN THE BUD

The easiest time to deal with cat aggression is before the behavior begins. There is one method that is excellent to use with kittens, while still permitting the owners to enjoy their kitten to the fullest extent. All kittens will playfully nip at fingers. But at each

New and old pets should be introduced to each other very gradually and only under direct supervision. Some cats and dogs may never get along.

81

Neighborly Advice

The hazards of the well-meant but inappropriate advice offered by friends and neighbors are exemplified by a case in which the owner had observed the beginning of aggressive behavior in her pet. She was advised by a relative to confine the animal to a dark closet when biting or scratching occurred. By the time I saw the animal, it was quite different from the friendly pet that had, prior to closet confinement, displayed some relatively minor aggression toward the owner. It was now withdrawn and fearful, urinating at random spots throughout the house, and openly hostile when the owner approached. This advice had been costly to the owner and the pet. The technique used to stop the initial misbehavior had actually increased the aggression, and other misbehaviors had appeared to further complicate the case. Furthermore, the owner's feelings toward the animal had quite understandably changed. It is very difficult for an owner to remain affectionate toward an animal that is no longer bringing pleasure, that inflicts wounds if she gets too close, and that increases housecleaning chores. When incorrect techniques are used, negative results are all too often predictable. In this case, it was a lengthy process to restore trust and affection in both the owner and the animal. If the owner had concentrated her efforts on winning back the cat's confidence before allowing the extreme aggressiveness to develop, the situation could have been avoided. She could have accomplished this through playtime, praise, petting, and lots of tidbits. Cats, like people, can be bribed.

instance of nipping, gently flick the kitten's nose with your finger. It is also useful to pair this finger flick with a firm command of "no." Your kitten will soon get the idea that this behavior is not permitted, while at the same time both cat and owner can engage in affectionate play. To combat excessive rough play, provide the kitten with furry toys or catnip-filled mice. Don't teach your kitten bad habits by playing games in which she bites or swats at your hand.

You can retrain kittens and older cats to be non-aggressive pets. Playing gently, stroking the head and face, and rewarding good behavior with food treats should do the job. There is no reason to ignore your kitten or turn her outdoors, and there are many benefits to be derived from a proper upbringing. Both animals and children need to know what is expected of them.

FIRST OFFENDERS

Very infrequently, cats have been brought to my hospital following a single aggressive act, with no previous history of such behavior. Happily, in most of these cases, I find that the isolated incident involved a bite as a reflexive response to pain, such as when a child had stepped on the cat's tail. However, the owners became frightened and immediately came to the clinic for aid. The most difficult aspect of working with these clients lies in calming their fears and persuading them that they do not have a monster on their hands. There is no guarantee that their cat will never bite again, for she most certainly will under similar circumstances, but a fearful owner may do more harm than good. Any act of aggression on the part of a pet should be of concern to the owner; however, if all available evidence seems to point to the cat's actions as self-defensive, any change of the owner's attitude and behavior toward the pet could produce true misbehaviors.

REDUCING AGGRESSION

Hold the cat down on her side for a few minutes several times a day. Only allow her to get up when you desire it. This procedure teaches the cat that you are dominant over her and that you are the boss. It sends an important message to an aggressive cat.

> ## How to Handle an Aggressive Cat
>
> - Never force your attention on her. Let her come to you.
> - Never try to pet her while she's lying on her back—an act that might provoke her rage.
> - When she hisses and growls at you, ignore her or fetch her toys to distract her. She may relieve her tension by taking her fury out on her playthings.
> - Never stare directly at her—it might be regarded as a threat. Never place your face too close to hers.
> - If a cat attacks you, grab the scruff of her neck (if possible) and hold her down while firmly repeating, "No! Bad cat!"
> - When retraining an aggressive cat, it is advisable to wear gloves and long sleeves.

Never play roughly with an aggressive cat. It overstimulates the animal and only adds to the problem. Be as calm as possible with this type of cat. In a very aggressive cat, it might be prudent to ask your vet about tranquilizers and hormones to help reduce an antagonistic attitude.

For overly aggressive tomcats, neutering will slow them down about 80 percent of the time. The additional use of hormones in neutered males will further reduce their aggressive nature.

CORRECTING AN AGGRESSIVE CAT

The best advice that I can give to you is to be cautious in disciplining an aggressive cat. They usually are overstimulated and can react violently to your overtures.

It is important for the cat to associate the word "no" with punishment. Whenever she bites your hand, say "no" loudly while slapping her gently but firmly. You can also gently flick your finger across her nose while saying "no." If she attacks your ankles, say "no" while using your foot to gently but firmly fend her off. In a short time, she will begin to associate the word "no" with a physical reprimand. Eventually, she will stop what she is doing or about to do when she hears the word "no." You must try to anticipate your cat's next move and say "no" to ward off any negative behavior.

TYPES OF AGGRESSION

There are many different types of aggression:

AGGRESSION AMONG MALES

This is the most common type of aggression in cats, and it can be helped 80 to 90 percent of the time by neutering. In some very aggressive cats, additional hormones and/or tranquilizers are required to take the fight out of them even after surgery for neutering.

PAIN-INDUCED AGGRESSION

Cats do not like to have their tails or hair pulled. That's why so many young children get bitten or scratched, because they don't know the cat's warning signals.

PETTING-INDUCED AGGRESSION

This type of aggression is seen in some cats that are being petted, when all of a sudden they scratch or bite. This reaction is observed in both males and females. In human terms, the offending cat is comparable to a person who has a sudden mood swing.

FEAR-INDUCED AGGRESSION

This behavior is seen when a cat cannot escape from an unfamiliar person or animal. Possibly involved are shy and timid cats that are cornered and cannot escape. They are very frightened and will lash out with a vengeance. Psychologists call this the "flight or fight" syndrome.

Aggressive dominance.

TERRITORIAL AGGRESSION

Such aggression is encountered when a new cat is introduced into a house and the other resident cats take offense to the newcomer. There has to be a long introduction period before the new cat will be accepted by the others. Behavior modification along with hormones and tranquilizers is needed to conquer this problem. Aggression can also be expected when a cat returns home after being gone for a while. He may show hostility by marking territory and by being aggressive toward his owners or any other cat or dog in the household.

HUNTING BEHAVIOR AGGRESSION

Some cats attack their owner's ankles in a simulation of hunting. This is usually seen in indoor cats between puberty and two years of age. Their hunting instincts take over and they use their owner's ankles as targets. To help correct this habit, carry a water gun to spray water in the cat's face. To discourage her from continuing this target practice, the owner should substitute other playthings. Other playmates or toys can help divert her attention away from your ankles. Excessive hunting behavior in indoor cats can be reduced with hormone therapy.

Medically Induced Aggression

This situation is comparable to the case of a person who has a headache and is not feeling well. The person is grumpy, and a cat can feel the same way, showing her feelings by biting and scratching. Two ailments that can cause a cat to bite are hypothyroidism (an underactive thyroid) and epilepsy.

Play Aggression

This is seen in overzealous cats that are very exuberant in their play. They get out of control and will bite and scratch when they are excited.

Learned Aggression

Some cats learn to bite their owners whenever they want attention, and unwitting people let them get away with it. This permissiveness can perpetuate the misbehavior, because the cat is not punished for it. If the owner squirted water in her face when she tried to bite, the cat would soon learn right from wrong.

Aggressive Dominance

Some people allow their cats to dominate them. One couple had a cat who was allowed to sleep in the bedroom with them, and he gradually took up a regular position on the bed. Soon afterwards, as his owners got undressed at night, the cat began to slap at them with outstretched claws, making his feelings clear—he wanted the bed to himself. The couple wound up moving into the spare room and giving their bedroom to the cat. This childless couple was parenting a cat instead of a child, allowing the pet to fill a deep void in their lives. When people are missing something in a human relationship, and their needs are not met, their pets can often get away with anything.

Jealousy-Induced Aggression

Another cause of aggression can be a cat that becomes jealous by association. A case in point concerns an eight-week-old kitten that joined a family that already had a dog in the home. The dog immediately took a dislike to the cat. The woman of the household would pick the kitten up and hold her while the dog tried to get at the kitten by barking and jumping up. The woman eventually had to let the cat go. No scolding or punishment would stop the dog from trying to attack. He was simply jealous of the cat. The cat learned to stay away from the woman because she associated her with the rough dog. The dog would not bother the cat if the husband were holding her, only when the wife was holding her. The cat began avoiding the woman whenever she could. At night, the cat climbed into the bed only if the husband went first. When the wife approached the bed, the cat would hiss and lunge at the woman, trying to scratch her. The cat just didn't want the woman in bed with the husband. The cat never did make friends with the wife, even after the dog died.

Stressed-Out Cats

Stress is a favorite catch-all word nowadays for explaining all kinds of disorders, from rashes to cancer. However, it is a real problem with real solutions. Stress is disturbing, and it triggers an immediate reaction, but it is not in itself the cause of behavior problems in cats. A normal cat will be able to cope with stress; a neurotic one will not. Most cats do not like loud noises, strangers, children who grab them, separation from their owners, or going to the veterinarian, but they can put up with these unpleasant events. A neurotic cat cannot. A stressful event will throw them into a fit of melancholy or ferocity.

Causes

Cats are creatures of habit, and any deviation from the norm can create anxiety and tension for them. Modern-day cats are faced with many more stress-inducing conditions than their ancestors were in the wild. Undomesticated cats could choose their own company and avoid environmental pressures. However, cats today are daily faced with many tension-producing situations that can generate illness and abnormal behavior.

Stress occurs in cats when they are faced with a frightening, perplexing, or unpleasant situation. Animals, as well as humans, react in a variety of ways to stress depending on their tolerance and their "boiling point"—that is, when they lose their cool. Some react mildly, while others become violent. A shy or timid cat will usually be affected by stress more than a cat with a stronger-willed personality. Most cats will react with a "fight or flight" response and will run away from trouble if they can. Escape is their first means of defense, but if they cannot evade the distressing predicament, they will fight. A cat has a short fuse—that is, she reacts quickly and instinctively to any situation that confronts her.

Cats in multi-cat families are especially vulnerable to frequent bouts of anxiety. These cats never know when they might be attacked, chased, threatened, or ambushed.

While many causes of stress in a cat are due to major changes in the environment, even a slight change in the soap used to wash her pan, toys, or blankets can cause a problem. A change in the brand of cat litter can cause tension. The cat is very sensitive and aware of the slightest variances in her environment. Anything out of the ordinary will be upsetting.

When a cat feels lots of tension, she may indulge in all types of misbehavior, such as spraying, indiscriminate house-soiling, destructive chewing, or scratching.

Severe emotional stress, anxiety, or shock can precipitate a loss of bowel or urine control in almost any animal. This is normal. However, there are mentally disturbed animals who lose bowel and urine control without any apparent cause. In such a disturbed cat, anything that is not to her liking can trigger these deviations.

There are innumerable reasons for a modern cat to feel tense. I will mention the most common:

- **Social Isolation** No contact with people or other cats.
- **Overcrowding** Too many cats together, as in a multi-cat family. Too many annoying people in a house.
- **Confined Environment** Living in a small area or locked in a cage (a form of claustrophobia).
- **New or Strange Environment** Moving to a new house or going to new owners.
- **Social Conflict** A new arrival in the house, animal or human. A transient stranger or a new baby.
- **Excessive Humanizing** Being treated as humans or surrogate children.
- **Loneliness and Boredom** Lack of attention from the owner.

A new baby in the house can cause stress and jealousy in a cat.

Abnormal Cats

- **Bereavement** Loss of an animal companion or the death of an owner.
- **Change of Location** Moving of a food dish or litter box.
- **Loud Noises** Uncommon and unexpected noises, prolonged exposure to high-frequency sounds.
- **Unpleasant Experiences** A trip to the veterinary hospital or boarding at the cattery.
- **Territorial Responses** Seeing a strange cat outside the window.
- **Exposure to Unfamiliar Environment** Travel by car or air.
- **Physical Problems** An overabundance of fleas or a debilitating illness.
- **Inconsistent Punishment** Scolding a cat infrequently and unpredictably.

Signs of Stress

Stress is manifested as irritability, anxiety, and/or depression. Like humans, cats differ in their response to a strain on their emotions and can react in a variety of ways. The most common signs of stress are as follows and can be seen individually or in combination:

- **Depression and shyness** (hiding)
- **Overaggression**
- **Excessive vocalization** Persistent crying and meowing.
- **Compulsive grooming**

Stress is manifested as irritability, anxiety, and/or depression. A stressed-out cat's facial expressions are unmistakable.

- Decrease in appetite or compulsive eating
- Dilated pupils (a look of tension)
- Indiscriminate house-soiling
- Tail-chasing
- Vomiting or diarrhea
- Panting excessively
- Sweating of the paw pads
- Self-mutilation (chewing on paws and tail)
- Psychosomatic illnesses Physical ailments that are emotional in origin, such as asthmatic-type wheezing.

Just as an unhappy person may often overeat, a cat may show emotional stress by compulsive eating. It is important to remember that stress can cause more than one symptom in the same animal—for example, withdrawal and compulsive overeating at the same time.

There are many types of replacement behaviors that seem to ease the animal's tensions. Some cats will start grooming themselves, licking their fur constantly, sometimes to the point of causing a skin irritation. During very tense times, cats will start digging or scratching anything within reach, often attempting to bury or cover up their food.

Environmental Changes

Cats are very astute in detecting emotional ups and downs in their owners and can become stressed if there is a lot of yelling, arguing, or crying in the household. Cats prefer to live in a happy atmosphere. One cat became a nervous wreck when his owners engaged in their frequent marital disputes. He would hide, shivering and shaking, from

Just like humans, a cat may react to emotional stress with compulsive overeating.

89

the loud voices and the various objects the couple threw at one another. No medication helped this cat until after his owners' divorce, when he settled down peacefully and quietly with his mistress.

Because cats are so aware of their owner's emotions, a person's fear reactions can intensify and compound behavioral problems in their animals.

A typical case of stress evolved as follows:

A complete personality change came over Brownie and Blackie when their house was undergoing extensive remodeling. Completely stressed out by the noise, confusion, and invasion of strangers, Brownie and Blackie changed from loving, playful companions to fearful, angry cats—hiding and breaking their previously perfect litter box habits, even hissing and striking out at family members.

I finally hit on a solution that restored the equanimity of the two troubled cats as well as all family members. Brownie and Blackie were moved into the relative peace and quiet of the familiar master bedroom. Their food and toys were moved into a convenient corner and their litter box into the bathroom. With frequent visits from family members for cuddling and playtime, Brownie and Blackie soon overcame their fears and returned to being the confident, playful companions their family loved.

Some cats are smart. They avoid stress by staying away. Bubba, an indoor-outdoor cat, began making himself scarce. He came home only to eat and then left again. Upon examining the situation, I realized that the cat was staying away because of the excessive noise and commotion in the house due to the addition of two adults and an infant.

Some cats can handle changes in the environment better than others. Particularly nervous cats fly off the handle and react drastically. Some of them hide, act either defensively or aggressively, and vocalize excessively. Some cats groom themselves as a sign of nervousness, and the excess grooming can cause all sorts of skin ailments. In many cases, a loss of hair is the only sign that is apparent. This disorder is more common in Siamese and Burmese cats or mixtures of these breeds, but it can occur in any nervous, "spooky" cat.

An interesting case is that of a house cat that lost most of his hair during spring and fall. Despite the attention of many veterinarians and much medication, the hair continued to fall out. Upon questioning the owner, I was told that the cat's main activity was sitting in the window watching all the activity outside. The owner told me that many cats came up to the window and scratched at the screens, which infuriated her pet. In these periods of excitement, the cat would lick himself furiously and intently. It occurred to me that this tension could be the cause of the loss of hair. My advice was to keep the cat from seeing any other cats outside, because this invasion of territory seemed to incite him to lick himself. The owner covered the windows with shades or drapes so the cat could not see the trespassers. This seclusion, plus doses of a mild tranquilizer, solved the problem, and the hair grew back within a short period of time. The cat's own territorial instincts had precipitated the anxiety that he suffered, which was more evident during the spring and fall breeding seasons when the tomcats were on the prowl.

Loud noises can be really upsetting to a cat. Doodles became a nervous wreck and the owners could not figure out the cause of the problem. It was revealed to me that the cat's owner was a trombone player and practiced every day in the house. The noise of the

One of the author's feline patients was so stressed by the outdoor cats he saw through the window that he pulled his own fur out.

Doodles became a nervous wreck when her owner played his trombone.

horn was driving the poor cat crazy. She hid under beds or in closets and would tremble most of the day, becoming lethargic and losing her appetite. The trombone player was advised to practice somewhere else.

Many cats get upset when they move to a new house. There are several things that you can do to ease the emotional pain of a new location. At the beginning, confine the cat to one room in the house so that she can adapt to that area and feel comfortable. Put lots of "security blankets" around the room to assure the cat of your presence. Towels and rags that the owner has frequently handled, emitting familiar odors, help give the cat confidence in her new surroundings. Gradually allow the cat to roam over the rest of the house, investigating every nook and cranny. This routine will help minimize the stress of the change of address.

Remedies—How to Cope with Stress

The primary objective in the treatment of stress is to reduce the cause of the tension. If you cannot find the predisposing factors quickly, and you need to calm the cat, confine her in a small, dark enclosure. This in itself will calm the cat, because she will feel secure. For further treatment, tranquilizers will help in desensitizing the cat during the process of behavior modification. Desensitization involves the repeated application of the problem-causing stimulus so that the cat gets used to the stressor gradually, while the tranquilization is reduced slowly until it is no longer needed.

It is important to remember that consistent routines and predictable surroundings minimize stress in cats. If you anticipate something that will bring about a change in the environment, such as a visitor or a trip, an anti-anxiety medication would be advisable for the fretful cat.

To a cat that is showing signs of anxiety, a calm and reassuring voice is very soothing to the cat's frayed nerves. The presence of a relaxed person is a good treatment for a stressed-out cat. When talking to tense cats, use their names as much as possible, because hearing their names relaxes them. They will respond to the tone of your voice and your body language. If possible, crouch down to her level when you are trying to relax a nervous cat.

Food is also good in reducing the anxiety in a cat by diverting her attention. Once you have a cat's attention, gently introduce her to the cause of the stress. Do it slowly so that she is exposed to the stimulus gradually while you are rubbing her behind the ears or under the chin. The cat may start to purr and forget her problem. It often requires much repetition before a cat completely forgets the agitating causes of the stress.

At times you may not be able to remove the cause of the tension, but you will diminish its effect on the cat if you will dish out lots of love, praise, and caressing. Soothing words work wonders. It is important to remember that cats can tell when their

One of the best ways to relax a stressed-out cat is to groom or pet her while softly talking to her.

people are uptight. The owner's nervousness is contagious. It is difficult for an owner who is jittery herself to calm a cat down. Before you handle an uptight cat, be calm yourself, even if you have to rely on transcendental meditation, yoga, or soft music.

There should be no noise or strangers around that might irritate an anxious cat. Soft music or the soothing voice of the owner on an audiotape is very good therapy for an uptight cat. Other ways of relaxing cats and diverting their attention from the sources of their stress are play periods with their owners and a treat of catnip. Some cats become relaxed when they are being brushed and combed.

One product available from your veterinarian in the form of a spray contains some of the properties of feline facial pheromones. Pheromones are chemical substances secreted by animals to mark their territory and communicate with others. This spray comforts the cat in an unknown or stressful environment (cage, car, boarding, new house, etc.) When transporting your cat in a cage, spray the product inside the cage a few minutes before introducing the cat. If the cat will be taking a car ride, spray in the cat's usual spot in the car. When boarding the cat, spray each corner of the cage before placing the cat in it. Repeat the sprays daily until the cat begins to rub her head in the areas that have been sprayed.

Also, your veterinarian has many drugs, hormones, tranquilizers, and sedatives, as well as anti-anxiety medications such as Prozac® to help reduce the tensions in your cat. However, these medications are not meant for long-term treatment. Finding out what is causing the stress and removing or modifying it is the treatment that gives the best results.

Neurotic Cats

"Is my cat crazy?"

I have been asked that question many times by cat owners who have endured an unending series of confrontations with their pet. Usually, there is a clash of personalities between the two. There is, in fact, a great similarity between cats and their people—they both consider themselves superior beings. This is where the clash of personalities arises. Also, because of their close association with humans, some cats eventually assume the idiosyncrasies of their owners, as we shall describe in this section of the book.

No, I do not believe that our beloved furry friends are crazy. However, they do have an independent spirit, a resourcefulness, and a charming lunacy.

Separation Anxiety

A lonely cat is an unhappy cat. Although cats are less likely than dogs to suffer from isolation, some dependent cats do suffer from being left alone for long periods of time. The average cat that is left alone for the day will find enough things to do to keep himself busy. However, the subordinate cat that dislikes being away from her owner is the one to suffer most from the pangs of loneliness. These companionless cats develop poor appetites, continually groom themselves, become sluggish, and oftentimes will show aggression. Many of these cats cry or meow a great deal until they get the attention or companionship they seek. Soon these cats learn how to get love by vocalizing, a behavior unwittingly taught the pet. (If you always pet her when she cries, she will learn to cry in order to get your attention.) On the other hand, some cats become depressed and apathetic when suffering from separation anxiety.

Cats are more likely to suffer from separation distress after prolonged periods of absence from their owners—several days or more. Some cats will show this same type of anxiety due to the loss of an owner or fellow pet. These grieving cats can react by refusing to eat, meowing and crying, acting restless or lethargic, and eliminating outside the litter pan. There are some cats that react to this anxiety by causing destruction in the house to relieve their tensions.

WHAT TO DO

Some of these cats can be cured by watching television. Many cats have been helped by a television set or a radio playing when they are alone. Seeing people or hearing their voices seems to be all they need. A case in point is Moxie, a very temperamental cat who hated to be left alone and showed his displeasure by becoming very destructive. He tore papers, rugs, curtains, and anything he could get hold of in his fits of rage. Eventually, I advised leaving the television set on, and it worked. Moxie became hooked on soap operas and began to watch the tube most of the day, no longer wreaking havoc in the house.

Moxie became hooked on soap operas and stopped wreaking havoc.

Other ways of keeping a cat from getting bored are to leave out plenty of toys or other objects with which they can while away the hours. Boredom leads to problem cats. For very depressed cats who hate to be alone, getting another pet for companionship works wonders in many cases. A kitten or young puppy that the cat can dominate is stimulating to a lonely cat. It is best to get a neutered cat of the opposite sex to avoid fights or other entanglements. At first there will be lots of hissing and snarling, but eventually the two of them will work it out and become good friends.

There are many ways that you can relieve and prevent separation anxiety in a cat by making her surroundings more stimulating. One way is to provide a securely screened or closed window to look out of. Birdwatching is one of a cat's favorite pastimes. She should have a high spot to perch on and plenty of toys to bat around. Another attraction for some cats is an aquarium. They can watch the swimming and darting fish for hours. Audiotapes of her owner's voice will also help a lonely, tense cat. One owner I know had a videotape made of herself talking directly to her cat in a soothing voice. She set the VCR to play the video several times a day to reassure her pet that she was nearby. It worked, and the cat ceased his destructive behavior during her absence.

A life-sized doll for the lonely cat.

One ingenious owner found an extreme solution that might work for you and your emotionally disturbed pet. Obtain a life-sized doll, dress it up in your clothing, and

The country cat that became a city cat.

daub it with your perfume or aftershave lotion. Seat the doll on a couch in the living room, and usually the cat will lie next to it, quietly and peacefully, instead of causing destruction in the house. When using the doll method, initially play a taped message of yourself, talking to the cat in a soothing voice. The scent, sight, and sound is enough to reassure the cat that her beloved owner is present. Eventually, the tape-recorded message should not be needed.

Nervous Breakdown

There are sensitive cats that can have "nervous breakdowns" because of overexposure to people. Hordes of people can really upset a nervous feline, especially a cat who is not used to seeing that many people. She will hide in closets and other dark places trying to avoid the crowds and the noise that goes with them. In a zoo in Japan, it was determined that the animals were highly nervous because of their round-the-clock exposure to people, so the zoo closed one day a week to relieve their tension. It worked. One patient of mine, a country cat, had a nervous breakdown when he moved to New York. All the noises of the big city literally drove him batty. The sounds of the cars, the honking of horns, and the multitude of screeching noises were too much for this cat from a quiet farm in North Carolina. He hid under beds or in closets, shaking most of the day. His appetite diminished to the point where he was no longer eating, and he resorted to all sorts of misbehaviors. No amount of counseling or tranquilization could salvage this cat's peace of mind until he was sent back to the quiet country life to which he was accustomed. The cure was instantaneous and he was a happy cat once again.

Mental Depression

Cats have emotional ups and downs very similar to those of people and may undergo periods of severe depression. A despondent cat may possibly be suffering from a physical ailment, a condition that could be determined by a visit to the veterinarian. If no sickness can be found, a thorough evaluation of the cat's environment will usually reveal some situation that could be causing the personality modification. The loss of a family member, either through death, divorce, or separation, can bring on emotional distress. The sudden disappearance of a playmate such as a cat or a dog can also cause a behavioral problem. Cats can be very sensitive to the fact that they have been abandoned by a loved one, whether animal or human. To be overlooked can also damage the tender ego of a cat. Being ignored by her busy owners can cause her to feel unwanted and unloved. Some sensitive and very social cats will suffer from depression and boredom if they are not given sufficient attention.

Adding a new kitten or puppy to a household can also cause depression in the resident cat. These felines will show a diminished appetite, loss of weight, and lethargy.

Cats also intensely dislike being subjected to loud noises of any sort. They sometimes frighten and dishearten cats into a depressive state.

SIGNS OF DEPRESSION

Any deviation from her normal behavior can indicate a depressed cat. Depressed cats are easily noticed because they hide in corners or under furniture. A depressed cat will usually hold her head down with her ears flattened as she slinks around the house. She

Adding a new kitten or puppy to a household can cause depression in the resident cat. This may pass when the two pets get used to each other.

A depressed cat may become lethargic, lying around and paying no attention to anything. She may stop grooming herself and be irritable. A trip to the veterinarian will help diagnose the problem.

may crouch, immobile, with her pupils constantly dilated. She may refuse to eat or groom herself and may urinate where she sits because she is too uneasy to move. A formerly playful cat may become lethargic, lying around and not paying attention to anybody or anything. She will also allow herself to become dirty because she does not groom herself. Furthermore, a dejected cat will not play with her toys and may not tolerate handling by her owner. An aggressive slap with her paw will let the owner know that she's in a bad mood.

Depression changes some chemical systems in the body, including several that are responsible for the sex drive. The condition is a major cause of low sex drive in both male and female cats, just as in their depressed human counterparts.

HOW TO HELP DEPRESSION

Early recognition of the problem is of the utmost importance. The longer the depression goes on, the more difficult it is to cure. The problem may be simple, such as the departure of a loved one, or can be more complex due to a complete changeover in the household. Once the cause is determined, the next step is to make things right for the unhappy feline. Whether it be the replacement of a dear-departed friend or a change of atmosphere in the house, the cat will quickly become aware of your effort to appease her.

Showing extra attention always helps a dejected cat. Playing with her, caressing her, and talking soothingly to her all help to allay her suffering. Another strategy that always seems to help is feeding her delicacies or tidbits of food. Presenting new toys helps some cats come out of their doldrums. Catnip also seems to be a pick-me-up. For an indoor cat that has been down for a while, a new experience such as a walk outdoors on a leash might restore her interest in life.

For the severely depressed cat, the use of antidepressant drugs, under the guidance of a veterinarian, is indicated.

Phobias (Fearful Behavior)

COPING WITH FEAR

Phobias are intense fear responses that are out of proportion to the real threat of a situation. For most people, fear of heights, fear of small places, fear of water, and other phobias can be conquered or at least alleviated with medical help. However, a fear-stricken cat is more difficult to treat due to her long memory and temperamental short fuse.

Things that can typically frighten your cat are as follows:

- Loud noises, such as those made by vacuum cleaners, motorcycles, trucks, thunder, etc.
- Noisy people
- Bells or phones ringing
- Sudden strange motions by people
- Strangers, either human or animal
- Riding in cars
- Hissing sounds
- Children

FEAR OF PEOPLE

A cat's fear of people is usually due to an improper socialization period when the kitten is most vulnerable, between four and eight weeks of age. If the kitten has had no contact with human beings before the age of 12 weeks, she will invariably be fearful of any person. A cat can also become apprehensive if she has been mistreated by people.

Some cats like women better than men or vice versa. Usually, the cat has had a bad experience with a man or a woman and holds it against that sex forever afterward. Any abnormal behavior in a person, either verbal or physical, will make a cat scared of that person. For instance, accidentally stepping on a cat's tail can cause a cat to foster a hatred for that individual. It will take a long period of desensitization to get the cat to accept that person again.

To retrain a cat that is fearful of strangers, a period of desensitization is needed to acclimate the cat to new people. With the aid of tranquilizers, cats can be made to feel more secure if they wear a collar or a harness while in the presence of strangers. They can also be permitted to remain in a cage while in the same room with these strangers so that they can see that no harm is meant to them.

The stranger can offer tidbits to help ease the tension, while talking gently and softly. The stranger should crouch down, stroke the cat gently on the head and face,

Fear of people is very common in cats that have been improperly socialized to people or mistreated. It is possible to overcome this fear with patience and consistent kindness.

move slowly, and never stare into the cat's eyes.

Eventually, with lots of practice, the cat will learn to tolerate new people. Even if she is not exuberantly affectionate, at least she won't run and hide at the sight of a strange person. In time, the scaredy-cat might even let an unfamiliar person stroke and cuddle her.

FEAR OF THUNDERSTORMS

Some cats are extremely afraid of thunderstorms and can get in a frenzy if there is a storm approaching. These cats hide in a corner or closet away from the noise and people. A cat like this usually prefers to be left alone during a storm, and if you attempt to comfort her or hold her, she will growl or bite you. These cats cry and shake until all the thunder and lightning subsides. Some sensitive cats will even react in fear on a normal rainy day because they are anticipating the sounds of a thunderstorm.

It has been noted by behaviorists that some cats that are fearful of storms have become that way by taking cues from their owners, who are also terrified of thunder and lightning. They simply copy their owner's neurotic behavior during a storm. One such owner and her cat would hide under the bed or in a closet, both of them shivering and shaking.

In the treatment of these phobic cats, some respond to food during the early stages of a storm. You should attempt to avert their anxiety attack with a choice tidbit of their favorite food. It may work if the cat is not very nervous, but in a very fearful animal, more serious methods are required. These ultrasensitive animals need to be desensitized to the sounds of the thunderstorm. You can obtain recordings of storms and play them to the cat in a very low tone at first, then increase the volume over a period of time, depending on the animal's reaction. All of the time that you are playing

Owner and cat hiding under the bed during a thunderstorm.

the recording, you should be giving the cat some juicy morsel of food in order to distract her from the fear-producing sounds. Do not reward the cat with food if she shows any anxiety about the recording. Stop the sounds and wait until the cat relaxes before attempting another session. Extreme cases of this fearful behavior can be helped with the use of anti-anxiety medication, which your veterinarian or animal behaviorist can provide, along with their good advice on how to proceed. It is wise to watch the weather reports and give a tranquilizer or other sedative to a nervous pet at the first sounds of an approaching storm.

FEAR OF THE OUTSIDE (AGORAPHOBIA)

If a kitten has been sheltered too closely all her life and has never been exposed to the outdoors, she might end up being fearful of the outdoor environment. Such cats prefer to stay indoors in the security of their homes. They tremble with fear when taken outdoors.

A fear of the outside world can also be caused by the memory of a traumatic incident in the past, such as a fight with a neighbor's cat or dog. The cat never again feels secure outside her home. Fortunately, cats can live indoors completely happy and satisfied.

WATER PHOBIA OR WATER FETISH

Most cats dislike water, but some nervous felines will react with violent anxiety to it or even to the sound of running water. These cats will make an effort to avoid being in the vicinity of any water, especially when a bath is imminent. Anyone attempting to give one

A cat that enjoys baths with his owner.

of these cats a bath will soon encounter the epitome of terror. These are the cats whose worst form of punishment is a squirt in the face with a water gun, an act which could possibly bring on an anxiety attack complete with hissing and unsheathed claws.

There is one cat I know that fears water so much that just the sound of running water in the tub or shower will cause him to run under the bed and hide, fearing for his life. Strangely enough, running water in the kitchen sink doesn't cause any emotional turmoil in this cat—probably because he has never had a bath in the kitchen sink.

By contrast, there are some cats that are fascinated by water and will jump into any water receptacle: tubs, pools, or even water holes in the backyard. Other cats can be found sitting in the sink batting away at a dripping faucet or drinking from it. Some cats will not drink from their water bowls, but only from a dripping faucet.

Some cats will actually jump into a tub while their owners are bathing and paddle around in the water. Other cats are so curious about water that they will creep up to the edge of the water, whether it be the tub or the kitchen sink, and stare into the water for long periods of time, occasionally swatting at or tasting some of the water. One ingenious cat cups her paws to catch small amounts of water, which she drinks.

One cat loves the flushing of the toilet bowl. He chases the water coming into the bowl by jumping on the seat and swatting at it.

Some cats will only drink water from a running faucet or what's worse, the toilet. If your cat insists on toilet water, keep the lid down whenever possible and don't use any harmful cleaners.

TREATING PHOBIAS

The treatment of any phobias, including those that aren't listed here, requires desensitization. The cat must become acclimated to the object of her anxiety. This is accomplished by gradually exposing the cat to the aggravating stimulus in increasing doses, while using medication to quiet her nerves. It is important to identify the things that make the cat fearful and prevent overwhelming exposure to these irritants.

The Over-Socialized (Dependent) Cat

Although it is wise to handle kittens as much as possible while raising them, some kittens become too dependent on their human companions. These overly sensitive felines suffer from behavioral derangement whenever they are separated from their "one person in the world." These overdependent cats become very agitated whenever they are left at home by themselves or when they are left in a boarding facility while the owner is out of town.

When left alone at home, these disturbed cats resort to many misbehaviors, such as forgetting their toilet training or otherwise getting into destructive mischief. If not destroying property, some cats ravage their own bodies by grooming themselves too much or chewing on their own skin until lesions appear. Other cats may overeat or go off their food completely. If your cat reacts emotionally when you leave the house, I would advise getting a companion for your pet. A young kitten or puppy may help divert their intense attention from you onto the new pet. If an additional pet is not practical, I would advise you to leave the radio or television set on while you are out of the house. Better still, I would advise you to make a tape recording of your voice and keep playing it for your lonesome pet.

When leaving these over-dependent cats at a boarding cattery while you are out of town, I would give the facility permission to use a mild tranquilizer for the cat to prevent a loss of appetite as well as the heavy anxiety that usually accompanies such emotional separations. One of my clients had a better idea. She brought in a large picture of herself and insisted that we hang the picture in her cat's cage so that he wouldn't get lonesome and forget her. Another cat lover called every day from Italy while on vacation so that her pet could hear her voice over the phone.

Psychosomatic Disorders

Psychosomatic ailments are a form of abnormal cat behavior. These illnesses are actual organic ailments caused by emotional factors. Although psychosomatic medicine is a fairly new field in veterinary medicine, help is available in many cases of emotionally caused physical disturbances. These animals are not faking a sickness. They are actually ill. Various emotionally stressful conditions are responsible for psychosomatic disorders, but the principal one is a change in the environment that is not to the cat's liking. Because cats are creatures of habit, any deviation from their normal routine can result in a stressful condition, sometimes an illness. Other causes may be jealousy, emotional problems brought on by loneliness, and sexual frustration.

One common psychosomatic disorder is a bronchial asthmatic attack, similar to that in a human. When the cat is upset, she can go into a series of spasmodic bronchial coughs that can be relieved by soft talk and petting to calm the animal. However, it should be remembered that most cases of coughing are due to actual physical causes.

Other cats with psychosomatic illnesses show digestive disturbances, including diarrhea or constipation, that can sometimes be cured by just changing the environment.

JEALOUSY

Jealousy is a very strong feline emotion and can result in psychosomatic illness. Some of the ailments are loss of appetite, vomiting, diarrhea, loss of hair, and asthmatic-like coughing and wheezing. There is a case of psychosomatic vomiting by a cat that was jealous of his mistress's boyfriend. Every time the man entered the house, the cat would start vomiting. Another cat had a personality clash with a person who was visiting her human family. This resulted in the closing of the third eyelid of one of her eyes. The eye resisted all medical treatment but went back to normal the moment the visitor left.

Another example of a psychosomatic ailment caused by jealousy is revealed in the story of a cat that developed a chronic skin disease that resisted all forms of normal therapy. After discussions with the owner, I realized that the skin condition did not surface until after a new puppy was brought into the house. After a test showed that the cat was not allergic to dog hairs, I realized the answer. The cat was simply jealous of the puppy, which was getting all the attention. In order to be noticed, the cat started scratching and biting herself until a genuine skin disorder resulted. The solution was simple. Getting rid of the puppy brought about a miraculous cure in a few days' time.

The jealous cat vs. the new puppy.

PSYCHOSOMATIC VOMITING

Some cats vomit whenever they are severely agitated. A high-strung, nervous cat can vomit whenever something bothers her.

There is a case of an overly pampered cat that vomited only when his owner was present. This smart cat knew that he would receive special love and attention when he vomited.

Another cat would vomit every time he saw the owner bring out the carrying crate. He knew that it meant a trip to the vet or a plane or car ride, none of which he enjoyed. To him it was a matter of life or death—or worse.

Treatment consists of desensitizing the cat to the disturbing influences. In these cases, drugs can be helpful in acclimating the cat to the source of the irritation and building up her confidence.

FALSE PREGNANCY

False pregnancy is an example of a psychosomatic ailment that affects the queen both physically and emotionally, and the abnormal behavior seems to be controlled by ovaries that have gone awry. The animal believes that she is pregnant and shows many of the symptoms of pregnancy, such as enlarged mammary glands (including production of milk), swelling of the abdomen, and appetite change. At "delivery" time, she shows hyperexcitability in the form of panting and trembling. Many of these queens go through labor pains at about the time they would normally be delivering. Often, the queen makes a nest and proceeds to protect her "kittens," which might be toys, bones, or other objects that she carries around in her mouth. She usually curls up with her "kittens" tightly snuggled to her breasts. Queens in false pregnancy have been known to adopt entire litters of real kittens, puppies, rabbits, squirrels, or opossums and have produced enough milk to raise them during their entire eight weeks of suckling.

Various symptoms of false pregnancy include restlessness, looking for kittens, whining and crying, scratching at rugs, and trying to make a bed for the "litter." Some cats instead may become quiet, go off their food, and curl up in a corner wanting to be left alone. Fortunately, with the cessation of the false pregnancy, the cat returns to her normal self.

In some queens with a strong maternal instinct, false pregnancy makes them more affectionate with their human companions. Others show their maternal frustrations by exhibiting extreme behavior, and there are cases of queens stealing kittens from other queens.

In the treatment of this ailment, hormones provide the best relief, and, if the animal is extremely upset, tranquilizers are beneficial.

HALLUCINATIONS

Occasionally, cats behave bizarrely—staring into the air as if watching an object floating around in space. Their eyes seem fixed on one particular spot when all of a sudden, they start running after this imaginary object until they pursue it over the entire house, knocking over anything that gets in their path. Eventually this helter-skelter chase stops as abruptly as it started, and the cat goes back to sleep or grooming as if nothing happened.

Most animal behaviorists believe that this type of hallucination is a remnant of the hunting instinct of years gone by.

Cat hallucinations.

DESTRUCTIVE CATS

There are very few bad cats, but there are thousands of mischievous cats. They really don't intend to get into mischief—they simply must investigate everything, and in doing so they can disrupt the order of your house.

Plants, drapes, sofas, chairs, and clock pendulums are among the common targets of a destructive cat. It is not unusual for cat owners, with reluctant resignation, to forgo fancy household furnishings, such as an upholstered sofa or luxurious philodendron. They may rationalize that shreds and tatters give a home a "lived-in look." So prevalent is the notion that to bring a cat into proximity with furniture and carpets is to invite ruin, that many apartment house owners refuse to rent to families with cats. Unfortunately, there is substantial support for this restriction.

Destructive Chewing

The cat's teeth are designed for eating flesh. They are, therefore, sharp and capable of remarkable gripping and tearing. One client, who had her cat declawed because of the sofa scratching, found to her dismay that the cat soon began tearing the sofa to shreds with her teeth. One of my suggestions was to spray a repugnant substance on a rag and pin the rag to the sofa. Through this and other recommendations, the sofa was saved from further abuse, and the cat was saved from losing her teeth. It is appalling to think of the number of misbehaving cats that undergo exodontia, the surgical removal of teeth. I do not condone this radical measure, because there are many gentler and more effective ways to modify behavior.

Destructive chewing is a misbehavior that can lead to the death of the animal if harmful materials are ingested. Household insulation, Christmas tinsel, and wool are targets for some cats. Insulation, in particular, can be extremely abrasive when it passes through the digestive tract. The cat, of course, should not be permitted access to these materials, but as is the case with wool eating, prevention is sometimes not possible. In such cases, spray repellents may help establish an avoidance response to ensure that the material is unattractive to the cat.

Other materials may be dangerously interesting to a cat that likes to chew. Shiny rings and watches are attractive, and cigarettes easily roll with the push of a paw. If

107

One dangerous habit that some cats enjoy is chewing on electric cords. To discourage this, rub vinegar or pepper sauce on the wire.

objects such as these are within the cat's reach, the owner may find tobacco strewn around the floor, or a favorite ring may not be found for months. It is wise to inform overnight guests of the cat's playful antics in order to circumvent a household search for a cuff link the next morning. Unemptied ashtrays are also subject to a playful paw, and some cats actually enjoy chewing on cigarettes. I have not found that cats are necessarily repelled by lit or smoldering cigarettes, and the hazard of sparks on flammable surfaces is obvious.

Another dangerous habit that some cats enjoy is chewing on electric cords. To discourage these cats, you can rub vinegar or pepper sauce on the wire. Both are very distasteful to a cat. To stop chewing on furniture or clothing, you can use a hot pepper sauce to intimidate the cat. First, let the victim smell the hot sauce, then squirt a bit into her mouth—an unforgettable experience. After that, whenever she smells the hot pepper sauce near any furniture or garment, she will avoid it like the plague.

The burden of responsibility for preservation of home, pet, and other possessions falls to the owner. With training, the cat will not walk on the kitchen table or sink and will not chew or hide articles, at least in the owner's presence.

Destructive Scratching

Because scratching is such a deeply ingrained, normal instinct in cats, its distressful consequences in a house full of modern-day furniture, rugs, and draperies are all too familiar to most cat owners. Indeed, scratching is the most common problem faced by cat owners. No amount of scolding or punishment will make the natural tendency to scratch go away.

Much confusion surrounds the act of scratching. Cats do not scratch simply to sharpen their claws. While scratching does condition the nails by removing the worn outer shell, it also serves as a muscle-toning exercise. The cat also scratches to mark her scent on the object, letting other cats in the area know that she has been there first. There are glands in the feet that leave a distinct scent mark on the target.

Declawing a cat will not stop the scratching behavior, and I have had clients with declawed cats who still complained of their furniture being destroyed by scratching. It seems that over a period of time, calluses had developed on the toe pads that were almost as effective at tearing as the claws had been originally.

SCRATCHING POSTS

Scratching furniture is a normal behavioral expression of an indoor cat, because she cannot claw on trees and posts on the outside. Therefore, you must discourage furniture scratching by providing an acceptable substitute. A scratching post is one of the most successful methods of dealing with the problem. If the cat is concentrating on one piece of furniture, cover it with a heavy plastic cover. Because she likes to sink her

Scratching posts often seem to be sized for kittens—many simply aren't tall enough for a grown cat to use.

claws into something soft, she will not enjoy scratching the plastic material. Place a scratching post nearby so that she can resort to that if the plastic displeases her.

Good commercial scratching posts are difficult to find. Somehow, they always seem to be built for kittens. Many cat owners purchase scratching posts, believing that they are well on their way to having a pleasing, nondestructive pet, only to find that within a few weeks the kitten has gone elsewhere for stretching exercises and the scratching post is knocked over in the corner. Be sure that the scratching post is a sturdy one so that it won't tip over and frighten your cat. If she seems nervous about a large upright post, lay it on its side so that it doesn't seem so tall and threatening. While outdoor cats find trees quite satisfactory, a scratching post or its equivalent is an absolute necessity for proper training of a kitten that is expected to live indoors. If an adequate one cannot readily be purchased, they are relatively easy to build. Some people are skilled in carpentry and build rather elaborate structures.

There are many types of posts, from those that are 12 inches high to those that extend all the way to the ceiling. Many variations have ladders and shelves spaced along the pole. There is a large apartment-like co-op that can house up to four or five cats comfortably. This "kitty housing project" is completely covered with carpet. A ball or other toy attached to the post can entertain a cat for hours, while allowing her to hit and scratch away all her frustrations. Most scratching posts are vertical, although some cats prefer horizontal posts. Be sure that the mat or post is long enough to allow the cat to stretch her body out fully. For a kitten, provide a scratching post near the kitten's sleeping area so she can get used to it. Install different types of scratching posts in

Several types of horizontal scratching posts are available, and some cats prefer them.

Good scratching posts are covered in both carpet and sisal and are of sturdy construction. They may also feature a dangling toy or catnip cup to tempt the cat.

several areas around the house. The post has to be convenient for the impatient cat, and installing one post in a large house may not be enough for a lazy cat. A very popular scratching device that is attractive to cats is a honeycombed corrugated cardboard box that is laced with catnip. Cats will scratch, roll on, rub, and even sleep on this material.

The texture of the scratching post covering is critical to whether or not the cat will use it. Most cats prefer loosely woven fabrics with a vertical weave that shreds easily, because the longitudinally running threads make it easy for the cat to drag her claws through it. Cats will tend to avoid posts with a tightly woven, nubby material that they can't drag their claws through. Other cats prefer posts with natural bark covering or sisal, which is a tough fiber used to make rope.

A scratching post should be available when the kitten is first introduced into the household, and it should immediately become a play object. The kitten should be taken to the post several times each day, particularly when there are any indications of scratching. It is also good practice during the first few weeks to take the kitten to the scratching post each morning. When cats first awaken, there is usually a period when they stretch and engage in other muscle-toning exercises, and this activity should be directed at a scratching post.

For some kittens, it may be necessary to demonstrate what the post is for by

111

Obstinate cats that ignore a scratching post may like to scratch small logs of wood placed around the house. Make sure the logs are clean and bug-free.

manipulating their front legs as though they were going through the motions of scratching. Other cats can be enticed to use a scratching post if you first rub catnip on the surface. Some people rub the smell of kitty treats onto the scratching post. Praising your cat whenever she uses her post encourages her to use it again. It is advisable to change the carpet on the post only if the cat loses interest in it. Cats tend to prefer worn post coverings to new ones, so don't replace the covering too often.

There are some obstinate cats that will not use a carpet-covered scratch post but instead prefer to sharpen their claws on doorframes, windowsills, and other wooden objects. For these cats I advise providing small logs of wood in the house for them to scratch to their heart's content.

Regardless of how the cat is discouraged from generalized scratching, she must be provided with suitable scratching post areas where scratching is not only permissible, but actually promoted. The best way to train a cat to use the post is to catch her scratching in the wrong place and immediately remove her to the proper area. This method is very effective with kittens, but it is less effective in changing the behavior of an adult cat. However, patience, repetition, consistency, and firmness should eventually pay off.

OTHER SCRATCHING REMEDIES

For those owners who end up with an unused scratching post and frayed household objects and nerves, there are a couple of things to try before resorting to the supposed cure-all, declawing.

When faced with a destructive scratcher, it is also important to clip your cat's nails at regular intervals. Shorter nails will cause less damage. The procedure is simple, and your veterinarian can teach you how to clip the nails safely. The earlier in the cat's life that you begin clipping, the less she will mind it. It takes an older cat longer to accept nail clipping.

Another technique that has proven effective in stopping the cat's destruction of furniture and plants is using a water gun. If your aim is good, a squirt of water when the cat is caught in the act can at least make her think twice before going to that spot again. The squirt of water should be accompanied by a loud shout, "No." Cats are not particularly fond of being hit with a stream of water. (*Do not* use the water gun with some other misbehaviors, such as urinating outside the litter box. It could start the cat's eliminating any place in the house, just so long as she is out of your sight—in your shoes or on your bed, for example.)

Correcting scratching with a water gun.

Do check your furniture and drapery material for resistance to water spotting before using this technique. An alternative to water is an air gun or a canister that contains air that can be squirted at the cat's face.

Some people have had good results with mothballs. These can be put into little cloth bags and placed in areas that the cat especially favors for scratching. Mothballs are also splendid flea deterrents, but they should be in a closed container, because they are toxic to cats when ingested. Cat repellent sprays may be effective, and underarm deodorant sprays are also useful in discouraging a destructive cat from using off-limits scratching areas. When deodorant is sprayed near her face several times and then applied to the piece of furniture, it will remind her that this is the same odor as on the forbidden couch and the area should be avoided. Citronella sprays are also helpful.

Balloons have also been used with some success. Any piece of furniture especially favored by the cat can be adorned with inflated balloons. Curiosity will entice the cat to the balloons. Inevitably, she will stab a balloon with a claw, and the resulting explosion usually proves startling enough to get the point across in short order. After this experience, one balloon can be placed in a strategic spot to indicate to the cat that the area is out-of-bounds.

Mousetraps have also been used to show cats that there are places off-limits to them.

Abnormal Cats

An upside-down mousetrap will not harm the cat but will scare her enough to jog her memory the next time she trespasses.

Another remedy is to put a lightweight object such as a tin pan or plastic dish on the edge of the targeted chair or couch. When the culprit attempts to scratch the furniture, the pan or dish will fall, making a lot of noise. If this happens several times, the cat will begin to avoid the furniture, especially if she sees a pan or dish on it.

Correcting scratching with balloons.

Researchers have found that cats learn more quickly by sound association and fear of that sound than by physical force and pain. For this reason, some animal behaviorists advocate various sound devices in the retraining of problem cats. There are many ultrasonic devices, shock mats, and infrared gadgets that detect vibration, all of which can be used to provide stubborn cats with an unpleasant experience.

Recently, plastic coverings for cats' nails have been devised by some ingenious cat lover. These coverings remove the threat of sharp claws doing any damage in the

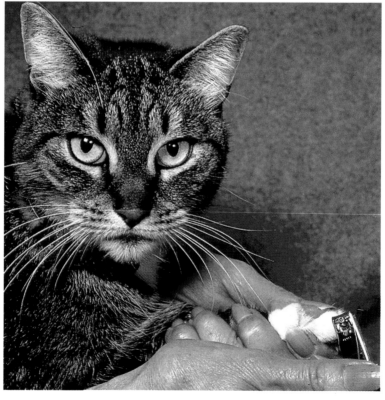

Declawing is not a foolproof measure for dealing with destructive behavior. It's a much better idea to clip the cat's claws regularly and train her to scratch only in appropriate places.

household but don't affect the cat in any way. These nail covers remain over the claws for an extended period of time and may be purchased from your veterinarian or at pet stores.

Psychic Trauma of Declawing?

Cat owners often question me about the possible psychological effects of declawing their pet. Declawing is not a cure-all, nor is it a foolproof measure for dealing with destructive behaviors. If, however, an owner wishes to have a cat declawed, there should be relatively little concern about possible detrimental psychological side effects. The cat will experience sore paws for a few days, but there is little likelihood of a sore ego.

There are precautions that cat owners must take if they have declawed pets. Such animals should not be permitted to roam freely outdoors. While only the foreclaws are removed and a cat may still be able to climb trees, these claws nevertheless are the first line of defense for a trapped cat. Without them, the animal may become easy prey.

Permanent restriction of a previously free-roaming cat may bring about a dramatic behavioral change that is not directly related to the surgery but that is perceived as such by an owner suffering from feelings of guilt. These guilt feelings give credibility to the idea of "psychic trauma" in the cat.

Another form of related guilt is rooted in the misconception that *all* cats need the freedom of outdoor life. This "need" to be outside actually develops only as a result of experience. Whenever a cat's life space is reduced, whether from the outside world to the house or from the entire house to certain rooms, personality changes must be anticipated. In other words, confinement by itself will not give rise to adverse reactions in cats that have been accustomed to a confined existence since kittenhood— provided, of course, that the confinement area is essentially equivalent to the family living area. Behavioral alterations resulting from a shrinking of the cat's world are not irreversible, but the process of converting an outdoor animal into a well-adjusted house pet will demand a generous amount of patience and understanding on the owner's part. These truths do not apply to bachelor tomcats. The instinctive sexual drive in these males will compel them to roam, seeking mating opportunities wherever possible.

CATS WITH LITTER BOX PROBLEMS

lthough cat owners ask for professional guidance in dealing with many feline misbehaviors, one of them far outranks the others in serving to prod owners into seeking professional help. When a cat stops using the litter box, owners are devastated. Few people have ever taught kittens to use litter boxes. This routine is part of the mother cat's basic training of her kittens. When a human acquires a kitten, there is little to be done, other than to show the kitten where the box is located. After the initial introduction, and provided that the distance from the box to where the kitten is at a given moment is fairly short, correct litter box use is not generally a problem. So if litter lapses do occur, the owner is totally unprepared to rectify the situation.

There are three basic classifications of cats that fail to use the litter box: the senile cat, the sick cat, and the environmentally stressed cat.

The Senile Cat

Senile pets have long histories of fastidiousness, but with advancing age, physiological changes lead to the loss of bladder and/or bowel control. Just as human beings may become incontinent, so do many cats. This loss of control is not an inevitable fate for old cats, but if it occurs, little, if anything, can be done about the incontinence itself. Instead, the owner must make litter boxes more accessible.

For an old cat, arthritis and other age-related problems can make it difficult and painful to get into a litter box, so it is wise to have shallow boxes that afford easy access. It is also prudent to install several more boxes around the house so the senior citizen doesn't have to walk as far to find a toilet area.

The Sick Cat

Cats in this group have litter lapses as a result of some physical disorder. During bouts with cystitis or bladder stones, for instance, a cat will excrete small amounts of urine at short intervals. If owners rapidly discover a cat's distress and get medical help from the veterinarian, there will be, as a rule, no subsequent changes in the cat's litter box behavior. However, if recognition of the ailment is delayed, there will be an almost inevitable breakdown of housebreaking. Urination is painful, frequent, and urgent, and the cat cannot always manage to reach the litter box in time. Many of these sick cats will excrete their bloody urine in sinks or bathtubs. If this behavior persists for an extended period, it often develops into a habit. This means that urination outside the litter box will continue after the physical cause has been medically treated and alleviated. Owners of these cats now have a job on their hands.

The Environmentally Stressed Cat

Cats exhibiting inappropriate elimination due to stress present the most challenging cases and undoubtedly the most exasperating for owners. The best descriptive term that can be applied to the cause of the misbehavior is "change." A change that is traumatic to the cat is often not perceived by the owner, and even when recognized, the owner views it as inconsequential and not a possible cause for the pet's inexcusable behavior. These owners often believe that their cat has suddenly become neurotic, a term too easily used as a catchall for undiagnosed misbehaviors.

An illustrative case, in which seemingly routine matters become overwhelming to a cat, was presented to me when a young couple came to the office with a two-year-old cat that had suddenly begun defecating and urinating in one of two rooms. The initial questioning brought assurance from the owners that nothing had happened to bring about the behavior. On the contrary, they said, the animal had quite inexplicably developed a full-blown neurosis. Careful inquiry, however, revealed that: (1) the clients had spent two weeks in Europe while boarding the animal for the first time; (2) a new kitten had been introduced; (3) the cat had been declawed; (4) a baby had been born; (5) the family had moved into a new house; (6) the husband's new commuting schedule had allowed him less time to spend with the cat; (7) workmen had been in and out of the house, and there had been general disorder during the month of the move; and (8) they had moved both the food dish and the litter box to a frequently trafficked bathroom. The owners had attempted some quite reasonable corrections but to no avail. In fact, their attempts had compounded the problem. None of the previous events had seemed significant to the clients. The clients were obviously bright, but working under the assumption that their cat was neurotic, they believed her behavior could not be readily understood or treated.

These stressful events had not occurred simultaneously. They had not even fallen within a short time span but had begun when the cat was eight months of age. The cumulative effect had eventually broken down the cat's resistance. A weaker cat would have succumbed much earlier in this chain of events. Once I had determined the causes, I was able to reinstitute acceptable elimination habits in the animal.

Certainly, the number of potentially traumatic events this cat encountered is atypical, but the basic pattern is common. If a previously well-behaved, physically fit pet starts using places other than the litter box, most assuredly *something,* not nothing, has happened. Ascribing the behavior to neurosis defines neither cause nor solution and interferes with the search for either.

It would be impossible to mention everything that might constitute traumatic change, but the aforementioned case presented several examples. Other reasons might be the

117

prolonged absence of a regular family member, the marriage or remarriage of an owner, or a new animal in the neighborhood that a cat can see, hear, or smell.

Basically, a cat's mood can cause changes in her litter box habits. A temperamental cat may be affected by even the slightest deviation from the norm.

KEEPING THE LITTER BOX CLEAN

Cats are creatures of habit and do not like any sudden changes, whether it be their diet, people or animals around them, or the smell of their litter. Changing the brand or type of litter may be enough reason for some cats to stop using the litter box. A dirty litter box is another deterrent to some cats.

CLEANING

The care of the litter box is of the utmost importance. Regardless of manufacturers' instructions on the bags of some brands of litter, claiming that the litter should not be disturbed between changes, I have personally obtained far better results by stirring up the filler. Many cats are fastidious animals; they will not eliminate in litter boxes containing even relatively small amounts of excrement. I have brought about a rapid and complete return to proper box use by instructing the owners of misbehaving cats to clean the box twice a day. This involves removal of solid waste, which can be flushed down the toilet, and stirring the litter, which hastens the drying process. If the litter is

For a highly nervous cat, determining the right spot for the litter box is very important. If the cat is frightened while in the box, she won't use it.

cared for in this manner, a total change of the litter and washing of the box is not usually required (for a single cat) more often than every two to four days, provided that enough litter is initially placed in the box. The box should be approximately three to four inches tall. Use a deep box so the litter won't be thrown all over the floor.

LOCATION

Be sure to place the litter box in a secluded, quiet spot, never in a noisy or high-traffic area. Cats are like people in that they want peace and quiet while they are at their toilet. A good place for a box for a shy cat is in the closet.

A patient of mine stopped using the box when the owners moved into a new home. When I visited the house, I realized what the problem was. The litter box was put next to the telephone, and the sound of ringing scared the cat as he was relieving himself. Cats are very obstinate and fussy about their toilet habits, and if they don't like the location of the litter box, they won't use it. If you ever have to move a box, do it slowly, moving it only a few feet every day. Cats do not like any drastic changes in their lives.

For a highly nervous cat, determining the right spot for the box is very important. A fearful cat is always thinking of an escape route if she is alarmed. For the cat's peace of mind, place the box in an area where a hasty retreat is possible.

CHOICE OF LITTER

The green litter containing chlorophyll has presented problems for many of my clients. This substance is supposed to eliminate odors in unclean litter boxes. Chlorophyll may well make the box more attractive to the owner, but it may also repel the cat. While some owners have had success adding some of the chlorophyll litter to the plain litter, the majority of my clients who have attempted even this partial change have had disastrous results. If the owner wants better odor control, a drop of liquid deodorant specifically sold for this purpose will render the cat box inoffensive to both owner and animal. However, there are some fussy cats that do not like any deodorants in the litter box and will consequently soil outside the box. An excellent product to use for masking odor is a thick layer of baking soda beneath the litter in the bottom of the box. This also allows for longer use of the litter, sometimes as much as two weeks without replacement.

Occasionally, seemingly minor changes in the brand of litter have brought about disuse of the cat box. If you are having a persistent house-soiling problem, allow the cat to choose which type of litter she prefers. Put out two or three boxes with different litters in them. Let the cat decide which one she likes. If she uses all of them, it means she isn't the choosy type, but if she only uses one box in particular, consider it the one of choice and disregard all the others. Some cats prefer noncommercial substances, such as shredded newspaper, sand, or cedar chips. Therefore, if a cat is misbehaving on paper, the litter box should be lined with shredded paper.

If a cat is properly housebroken, the wise owner will maintain the status quo. In other words, if it's not broken, don't fix it.

If more than one cat resides in the household, more than one litter box might be

119

advisable. It is also wise to remember that if you have a lazy cat, you should place several boxes around the house so the pet won't have to walk too far to get to a box.

THE ECCENTRIC CAT

There are some cats that are idiosyncratic about using their litter boxes. One cat I know will only urinate on paper towels placed in a box but will use another box with kitty litter in it to have his bowel

Sneezy doesn't like to get her feet dirty.

movements. If you are having problems, try using two boxes for your fussy feline. Other cats will not enter a covered litter box, while others prefer a smooth surface without any litter at all in their box. For cats that prefer to make a mess on rugs, you can use pieces of rug in the box. However, you must wash and replace the soiled pieces of rug at least every other day. For very fastidious cats who do not like to dirty their paws in certain types of litter, you can tack up a piece of rug on the wall next to the litter box so that the cat can scratch the carpet. This cleans her paws and exercises the scratch reflex, which keeps the cat's claw muscles in good working order.

I knew one temperamental cat that would only use the outdoors for his eliminations in good weather. On wet or nasty days, the cat would come in and mess up the house. He preferred not to use a litter box inside the house. However, his owners went through a long and tedious retraining program before they finally taught him to use the box or not be allowed in the house.

Sneezy is a very meticulous cat, almost to the point of eccentricity. She doesn't like to get her feet dirty with the litter in the box, so she resorts to all sorts of acrobatics when she has to eliminate. She stands on one edge of the box with all four feet and attends to nature in that position. She never enters the litter box itself. Sneezy is such a clean cat that she will attempt to cover with her paws any food or small object that is dropped on the floor.

On the other hand, there are some cats who are obsessed with litter boxes to the point that they will sleep in them and keep all other cats out of their private quarters. If one of the other cats should use their box, they go in and tidy up the premises.

GETTING RID OF THE BOX

Some people have humanized their cats to the point of training them to use the toilet bowl. There are training videos and Web sites geared to this technique if you are so inclined.

Some cats have learned to use the toilet instead of the box.

People Causing Problems

Cats understand much more than we give them credit for. They are strongly affected by their environment and the people around them. A good example of this is the story about a cat actually taking sides in a family argument. Mort, a well-housebroken cat, suddenly started leaving messes in the husband's study. It was about the same time that the husband and wife were having marital troubles and were fighting most of the time.

The people closed the study door only to have Mort mess up in the hallway outside the study. The owners tried every remedy. None stopped Mort's misbehavior.

After they consulted with a veterinarian who specialized in behavior problems, it was apparent to the professional that there was a lot of animosity between the husband and wife, and this was the reason that Mort was messing up the husband's room. He loved his mistress and was trying to punish the man in the only way he knew. The doctor's advice was quite simple: Kiss and make up. The people followed the advice, and within a short time, Mort became the fastidious cat that he once was.

There is an interesting case that illustrates how sensitive a cat is to minute

Mort took his mistress's side in every argument.

details. Sensitive to changes of any kind, Miss Puss suddenly started soiling outside her litter box. While being questioned about any possible changes in the household that might have caused such action, the owner suddenly realized that she had recently switched to a new perfume. To the cat's sensitive nose, her owner no longer smelled the way she always had. The new scent provoked the misbehavior, and either the owner had to go back to her old perfume or acclimate the cat gradually to the new scent. So she wore a combination of the old and the new perfume, gradually phasing out the old one. Miss Puss finally got used to the new fragrance and behaved properly once more.

Spiteful Urination

Sometimes a cat will urinate on an object belonging to one individual in the household. It usually signifies that there is a clash of personalities. Oftentimes, after severe punishment by the owner, a cat will urinate on that person's bed or on some clothing belonging to that person.

One cat dislikes the husband so much that he will urinate on his clothes or his shoes or defecate on his side of the bed. It is obvious that the cat and the human have to make peace with one another. That person has to show affection and give lots of attention to regain the cat's confidence and friendship. However, it does not mean that you should allow a cat to get away with any misbehaviors without being reprimanded. For naughty cats, some form of punishment is very important in order to prevent the mishap from occurring again.

One cat, Tomboy, shows his anger in a peculiar way. Whenever he is unhappy about something or someone in the house, he will urinate in his water bowl. He is one cat who likes to get his own way. If the owners sleep too late in the morning and don't let him outside, he will spray in the water bowl. If he doesn't get fed on time, he will head for the water bowl. He has his owners trained just the way he wants them. If they don't do as Tomboy likes, they have a soiled water bowl to clean.

Housetraining Tips

Before beginning any treatment for misbehaving cats, it is necessary to fully understand all aspects of the house-soiling problem. For instance, if a cat soils outside of her box, and you pick her up and throw her in her litter box, she will soon associate this with a form of punishment and will avoid the box even more. Never force a cat into a litter box while you are mad and yelling. It will frighten her and she will jump out as soon as possible.

When retraining a cat to use a box, reward her with a tidbit and some kind words to show her that she has done something good. The combination of the two—food and compliments—works much better than either one by itself.

If there is one spot in the house that the cat is soiling, put a litter box nearby so it is convenient for her to use it. Also put her food and water dishes on that spot to discourage her from misusing the area. Cats will usually not soil areas where they eat or sleep.

Do not put food or water bowls too close to litter boxes. Some cats will consequently avoid their boxes. It is wise to keep the food, litter box, and resting areas completely separate.

Make the litter box more attractive and convenient while making the soiled area less appealing. For the cat that has everything, you can install potted plants around the box for more privacy. Some very sensitive cats prefer to eliminate in an enclosed area, such as under furniture, in a small closet, or in a large cardboard box open only on one side.

If there is one location that the cat is soiling, turn it into a play area after a thorough cleaning. Put lots of toys on top of a plastic runner to cover up the soiled area.

Plastic mats can be used under litter boxes—some cats like the feel of the mat before they get into the box.

Covered litter boxes tend to trap ammonia, and some cats that are repelled by this odor will refuse to use the boxes.

Some stubborn cats will not walk on slick tile or a polished wood floor to get to their litter box. They usually prefer carpeting, so you may have to move the box to a corner of a room that is carpeted.

Plastic carpet mats can be used on areas that are frequently soiled, after a thorough cleansing. A soiled carpet retains a scent that attracts the cat, making her return to the same area for further eliminations.

If a cat is very persistent in soiling one particular area, put a chlorine-based household cleaner or a vinegar solution on a plastic sheet covering the soiled area. The odor of chlorine or vinegar will usually turn the cat away from that spot. Something else that cats dislike is the odor and taste of isopropyl alcohol. You can leave cotton balls soaked in alcohol in an area to deter cats from soiling there, but a daily spraying of alcohol is needed for several weeks as a reminder.

If a cat is soiling in only one particular room, close the door to that room because there is something in that area that is provoking the misbehavior.

Some lazy cats need several boxes spread around the house so they don't have to walk too far to get to a box.

Pain or anxiety associated with using the litter box will frequently cause a cat to eliminate elsewhere. This is usually witnessed during and after a bout with kidney or bowel infections. It can also occur if the cat has had a traumatizing experience in a litter box, such as being tormented by children or dogs or given medication.

In multi-cat families, one cat may be ambushing another while the victim is in the box, causing the cat to find other places for her to relieve herself. Watch a cat in the litter box. If she suddenly stops in the middle of urination or defecation, it could be a medical problem such as cystitis or constipation.

There are some cats that prefer to use bathtubs rather than litter boxes. Look at the urine closely to make sure there is no blood in it, an indication of cystitis or urinary stones. If the urine is clear, the culprit is simply misbehaving. This habit can be broken quickly by adding a few inches of water to the tub.

Sometimes it is difficult for a human to detect urine on rugs or other surfaces except by the odor. In rare cases, fluoroscein dye, which is excreted by the kidneys, can be given to the cat. Then, with the aid of an ultraviolet light in a darkened room, the soiled area will become very apparent. This method works well in a multicat family when you don't know which cat is messing up. Cats that urinate or defecate on the bed or clothing after an owner returns from a trip are using the marking behavior to show their displeasure.

If a new object is brought into the house and the cat urinates on it, clean it and then cover it with an old blanket or towel that has the scent of the owner on it. Usually a cat will not urinate on an object that smells like the owner. Remember, a cat does not like any changes. She likes things the way they always were. Any sudden change can trigger a stress-induced response.

A frequent provocation of inappropriate elimination occurs when an outdoor cat is not allowed to roam anymore and is turned into an indoor cat. These cats usually rebel against this new confinement, and much retraining is needed to convert these vagabonds into faultless house pets. If the cat is targeting a specific area, you can set booby traps to discourage the misdeed. Inflated balloons work well to remind Kitty that she is off-limits. Upside-down mousetraps and bags of mothballs will also refresh her memory. Ingenious owners have installed all kinds of electronic gadgets that will scare the cat but not harm her.

Don't punish your cat for mistakes. She will probably still avoid the litter box and may develop additional behavioral problems.

Never, never "teach your cat a lesson" by rubbing her nose in urine or feces.

123

House-Soiling Remedies

In any type of treatment for house-soiling, always try to determine the cause of the misbehavior. Preventing the cause of misdeeds always gives better results than treatment. Sometimes it is difficult to know what motivates cats to soil a house, so in order to find out, you have to endeavor to think like a cat. Once you determine what has precipitated the stressful condition causing the house-soiling, you can concentrate on modification of the behavior, using supervision and confinement procedures.

Whatever remedy you try, don't be too hasty in abandoning a form of treatment. Give each method at least a two-week trial period. Never try more than one remedy at a time, because you won't know which one works if you are successful.

Correctional Procedures

The first step is a thorough cleaning of the house, so that urine odors will not lure the cat back to certain spots. Many owners believe they have accomplished this feat, but they find to their consternation that the cat has begun urinating in even more areas than previously. Their choice of an ammonia-based cleaning agent was the fatal flaw in their otherwise commendable approach. Ammonia is a component of urine. Their cleaning, therefore, served to spread the odor over greater areas—hence, to the cat,

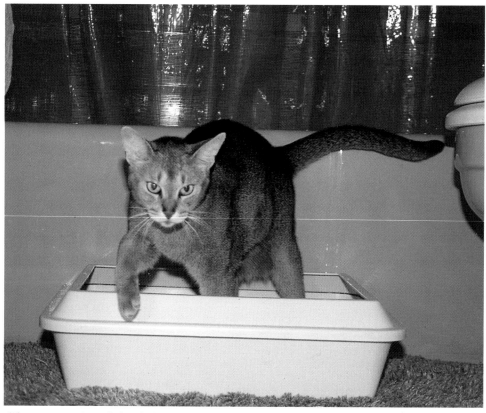

When you are not home, isolate the house-soiling cat with food, water, and a litter box in a room that has never been soiled. Do not allow the cat unsupervised freedom in other areas of the house until she begins using the box properly.

the house became one huge litter box. After cleaning with the proper substances, the area should be rinsed well with a dilute vinegar solution to mask the odor.

In some instances, cats have returned to regular litter box use following proper housecleaning. More often, the owners must initiate other cleaning procedures. Use of these additional cleaning techniques depends on numerous factors, such as the physical plan of the home, the number of people and pets in the household, and the time available for owners to devote to correctional procedures. Close supervision of the pet is advisable whenever possible, and if you catch her soiling outside the box, a loud noise or an object thrown in her direction will scare her enough for her to get the idea. Only use this procedure if you catch her in the act, or no more than a few seconds afterward.

When you are not available to supervise, isolate the animal in a room that has never been soiled before. Provide food, water, and a litter box. Do not allow the cat freedom in other areas of the house until she begins using the box properly. Do not allow her admittance to areas that have been previously soiled for at least several weeks so that all vestiges of odors are completely gone.

Accidents next to the box are the most common manifestations of house-soiling and are usually easiest to correct. Changing the type of litter, type of box, or the location of the litter box will usually prevent these accidents. However, don't overlook the type of disinfectant or soap used to clean the box. Some odors are objectionable to a cat, and simple sanitation can cure many a problem feline.

Some cats will urinate in front of the owner to gain attention. The cat feels neglected, possibly because the owner is not home as much as he used to be and not playing with his pet as often as in previous times. The best treatment in these cases is to pay more attention to the neglected feline. She is jealous of the owner's other activities. Playing with the cat and showing more affection will bolster her diminished ego.

Most cats soil a particular area and will usually return to the scene of the crime. If this is the case, you can use the following methods to divert the culprit:

Cover spots with aluminum foil or waxed paper, because cats hate the crinkly sound when they walk on it. Double-faced cellophane tape can be used over a frequently soiled area, because cats dislike sticky stuff on their paws. Another method to try is to put the food dishes on the spot that is soiled (after a thorough cleaning).

Plastic sheets sprinkled with chlorinated water will deter cats from walking on a surface, because of the smell and the fact that cats do not like to get their feet wet. Plastic mats can be used to cover an area after it is washed down with vinegar and water, and to further discourage the pet, leave a vinegar-soaked rag on the plastic covering.

Methods for Housetraining an Obstinate Cat

The following methods are not easy but are worth a try after ruling out all other reasons for the cat's stubbornness.

Confine the cat to a small room or a very large crate. Cover the entire floor with a thin layer of litter. Once a week, make the area in which the litter is spread on the floor smaller. Eventually, remove all the litter except that in a box. If the cat has no accidents outside the box for one week, you can release her from her confinement and allow her freedom in the house. Be sure to put several boxes around the house to remind her what the boxes are there for.

Fecal House-Soiling

Constipation, diarrhea, or impacted anal glands can cause a cat to defecate outside the litter box. In such cases, a medical evaluation by the veterinarian is necessary to rule out physical causes of the mishaps. A constipated cat will have a painful defecation, so it is important to be aware of the amount and consistency of the stools. A dryness of the feces means that more moisture, a fecal softener, or a change in diet is necessary. Adding liver to the diet will usually loosen the stools. When a cat is straining for a bowel movement, she is liable to move out of the box during the attempt. You should add additional boxes to make it more convenient for a cat that is either constipated or has diarrhea.

Impacted anal glands can cause pain during defecation and can cause cats to scrape their bottoms along the rug in order to relieve their affected glands. Professional help can readily correct this house-soiling problem.

It is important to remember that if a cat feels threatened, she may make her mark with feces. An aggressive, outgoing cat may also mark her territory with feces, but an insecure cat is more likely to spray. A cat may also leave feces uncovered in a litter box as a message to other cats, a form of marking behavior.

Ridding an Area of Odors

Various products are available to reduce urine odors in the house. These products either eliminate or absorb the odors. There are also enzyme-type deodorants that chemically decompose feline urine and dispel the odor.

If none of these products are accessible, it is wise to give the soiled area a thorough cleansing with a vinegar-water solution to neutralize the urine. The smell of vinegar is quite repulsive to a cat and she won't usually return to that spot.

Another good mixture for persistent odors is that of baking soda and aquarium charcoal spread over the soiled area. Leave it in place for a few weeks, and it will usually remove pungent odors. In fact, of all the deodorants available, tried-and-true baking soda gives consistently good results. For strong odors emanating from the litter box, you can line the bottom of the box with a thick layer of baking soda.

The use of many cleaning agents and disinfectants will increase the likelihood of urine-marking by the cat. Never clean soiled sites with detergents (or their derivatives), or, as previously mentioned, ammonia-based cleansers.

Using the Yard as a Litter Box

Some cats use the areas around the outside of the house as a litter box, with a resultant bad odor. Sprinkling a light coat of farm phosphate fertilizer on the soiled area will help control the odor. Cats generally dislike mothballs, and a few mothballs placed under the shrubs will probably discourage further misuse. If nothing else works, you can keep an uncovered sandbox in the yard that the cats would prefer to use rather than the dirt under the shrubs.

Medical Treatment of Inappropriate Elimination

Medication is not the final answer for house-soiling problems. Problems are more easily solved once the underlying cause is discovered and then corrected. However, veterinarians have at their disposal a variety of hormones and drugs that can be given to eliminate the problem. Even the human wonder drug for depression, Prozac®, has been successful in treating cats.

To Punish or Not to Punish

In correcting cats for litter lapses, *do not* punish your cat. She will become hostile, will avoid your company, and will still eliminate outside the box. *Never* rub your cat's nose in his urine or feces when he eliminates outside the box. In addition, *never, never* hit a cat to punish her for house-soiling—or for any other misbehavior for that matter.

Spraying (Marking)

Spraying with urine is an innate feline behavioral trait that in effect advertises the cat's presence. Spraying is the spurting of a malodorous substance on various household articles such as rugs, sofas, and drapes, while the cat continues to use the litter box for ordinary elimination. The foul-smelling spray essence consists of urine combined with a highly scented fatty substance. This act may serve to mark territorial limits, may be social in nature, and may occur under stressful conditions. Spraying is primarily practiced by males and, while normal, is perfectly dreadful. Spraying tends to increase in the courting male, indicating his sexual role. Unneutered males—particularly those confined in the house—and even female cats may spray anytime and anyplace, depending on the mood they're in. While males may do it continually, females often spray when they are in heat to allow tomcats in the area to know that they are receptive to mating. Sexually frustrated cats of either sex are usually the worst offenders.

Since spraying is primarily associated with sexual behavior and is an integral part of the mating act, neutering is the logical treatment. If a male begins to spray prior to neutering, the behavior may continue for an extended period of time. Although neutering a male that has never sprayed is generally an effective means of preventing the act, it does not guarantee that the behavior will not occur under traumatic circumstances. Stress in the environment may trigger spraying, even in the neutered male with no prior history of such behavior.

Some tomcats never spray. This is a sign of a reduced libido and a lowered level of blood testosterone, and these tomcats are usually unsuccessful in mating and producing offspring.

If you have ever experienced the odor of spraying, you know that this behavior must be prevented. If a male cat is intended as a house pet, have him neutered. If the male is to remain intact, be prepared for indoor infractions. Whenever changes are to take place within the household, introduce the cat to these changes gradually, and provide the pet with an abundance of tender, loving care.

Spraying is a marking behavior that can be heightened by any stressful situation confronting the cat. A few conditions that precipitate spraying are decreased attention

A reaction to threatened territory.

by the owner, excessive punishment by the owner, overcrowding, introduction of a new cat, and any change in routine. Spraying is more common in multi-cat families than in a home with a single cat.

Emotionally induced spraying near windows may occur in a normally clean cat that is used to perching in windows to watch cats and other animals on the outside. Obviously, these animals outdoors annoy the cat, because he thinks that his territory is threatened. To alleviate stress, the cat must be confined to a room in the house where he cannot see out. This isolation, along with the odor of his own hair and dander instead of urine, reinforces a feeling of security. Tranquilizers and hormones may also be given to help calm the agitated animal. Gradually, over a period of time, the cat may be allowed to enter other parts of the house, but the only windows that are allowed to be used as observation posts should be those out of which no roaming animals can be seen. It should be noted that outside cats are more noticeable during the mating seasons, and this is the time of the year when we see more spraying incidents with indoor cats.

Some cats have a very annoying habit of spraying on any new person entering the house. Such a cat sneaks up and sprays on that person's leg. Either the cat is marking the person as his territory or else he is showing his disapproval of the person, possibly because the smell of a nonresident animal is on the visitor.

Most cats are very observant, and their owner's actions may bring about spraying. There is one highly intelligent Siamese that sprays whenever he sees his owner packing a suitcase. He associates the suitcase with being left alone or going to the boarding cattery. To show his indignation, he usually will spray the suitcase as well as other strategic places in the house. To outsmart these cats, it is best to pack the suitcase out of view of the cat. Some spraying cats are so smart that if the owner screams at them

Spraying the owner's suitcase.

when they catch them in the act of spraying, they will usually only spray when the owner is not present. After an especially nerve-wracking incident, some high-strung cats will spray in order to relieve their tension.

Sometimes a territorial dispute between two cats in the same household can precipitate an outbreak of spraying. In one case, two altered male cats lived peacefully together until suddenly a large amount of spraying was going on. Neither cat was caught in the act, but one of them had begun rubbing everything and everyone while drooling profusely. Urinating outside the litter box and exuberant rubbing of the head are both signs of territorial marking behavior. Even though the two cats did not fight, these behaviors may have been a sign of a territorial dispute. Many cats simply do not want any other cats around and display these behaviors to warn other cats that this is their territory. Jealousy is a strong feline emotion and very difficult to assuage. In the case of the drooling cat, medical intervention was necessary. Hormones and tranquilizers were helpful in soothing the pair's territorial instinct.

The marking behavior is usually associated with odd places in the household. Cabinets, beds, closets, countertops, drapes, and all types of furniture are likely targets for marking. Some cats will spray on shoes and clothing because it has the scent of their "people." If there are any new articles brought into the house, they could be future targets for the cat. When moving into a new house, some cats will spray in order to get their scent all over the household. One sensitive cat disliked the odor of a wall-mounted heating unit in the new house and proceeded to spray on it profusely to cover the scent of the heater with his own.

Some cats make their mark by defecating. One such cat would greet his owner on his return from a trip by defecating on his bed. Possibly this was to show the owner displeasure with his absence, or the cat may just have been marking the bed with his feces. Most cats will show their indignation about their owner's absence after the owner returns home rather then while he is away.

Scientists aren't exactly sure why cats target certain people for marking mishaps. Most people think a cat marks the belongings of a person she dislikes, but there are many instances of a cat choosing a person of whom she is usually fond. Researchers have determined that an insecure cat, or one that feels threatened, is more apt to spray, whereas an aggressive, outgoing cat marks his territory with feces.

Is it Spraying or Indiscriminate Urination ?

There is a difference between spraying and urination, and this is important when determining the cause and subsequent treatment of cases of indiscriminate elimination. Urinating on a vertical surface away from the litter box is usually a marking behavior. Urinating on a horizontal surface is usually elimination but on occasion can be marking.

When a cat is urine-marking, he or she quickly squats with tail jerking and hind feet treading. If a cat takes her time and exhibits digging and burying behavior, she is usually in the act of elimination.

If a cat is house-soiling in addition to using the litter box, it usually signals a marking mishap.

If a cat is urinating and defecating in the same spot, it means that he or she is using it as a toilet area and not a marking spot.

The posture of a cat during normal urination is important to note so that you can

Urination vs. spraying.

differentiate it from the posture of spraying. In normal urination, the cat assumes a posture almost like that of a sitting position, back legs slightly spread with tail pointing backward. When a cat is in position to spray, he stands with his tail standing straight upward and quivering. The front part of his body is lower than his rear, and the urine is ejected upward to reach the object.

REMEDIES FOR SPRAYING

First and foremost, neutering the animal, whether it is male or female, will help in most (but not all) cases.

If a specific area of the house is being sprayed, a thorough cleansing with an enzymatic cleaner that completely absorbs odors is in order. Close off areas that are being targeted. Attempt to discourage the cat from using that area by using foul-smelling sprays and other frightening objects. There are all kinds of electronic gadgets that can be rigged to scare the cat away, or a simple upside-down mousetrap will serve the same purpose.

Another method is to put toys or a food bowl filled with dry food in front of the soiled area, even if the cat doesn't eat dry food. Cats are reluctant to spray on their toys or their food bowls.

If a cat sprays in one specific area, you can put objects on the floor to discourage her from using that spot. Plastic, aluminum foil, or possibly a cookie sheet with water on it will help, because cats hate to get their feet wet.

A feline pheromone spray available from a veterinarian can also help to reduce or prevent urine-marking. It is sprayed directly onto the places the cat has soiled as well as on prominent nearby objects. The spray is applied daily until the cat rubs her head on the spots, marking them with her own pheromones. This chemical substance helps the cat familiarize herself with the environment and thus reduces her stress.

There are also psychoactive drugs and hormones that can help, along with behavior modification techniques to rehabilitate chronic offenders.

CATS WITH BAD HABITS

When a cat picks up a bad habit, there is usually a logical reason for it from the cat's point of view. It is important for the owner to try to understand why the pet is being "bad." Cats usually don't misbehave out of spite. If the owner understands why the cat is behaving in a certain manner, he might be able to help with a retraining program. Even the most annoying feline habits can usually be overcome with a little patience and understanding.

Waking the Owner at Night

Cats are nocturnal animals; they instinctively sleep through the day and hunt at night. If your cat keeps you up at night, there are ways of combating this problem. However, if you get out of bed to feed her or play with her or even just to scold her, you are reinforcing her nighttime shenanigans by giving her the attention she is seeking. Because of this, the misbehavior will likely continue.

A cat may try a variety of ways to wake you at night. She will meow, knead on you, walk on you, bump you with her head, or insert her cold nose into some sensitive part of your anatomy, such as an armpit or behind your knees. There is one cat that wakes his owner up every morning by licking the person's eyelids until she opens her eyes. Shutting these cats out of the bedroom often will not work, because they will meow loudly until you respond to them.

Discipline has to be firm enough to let your cat know that you are irritated by this kind of behavior. A flick of your finger on her nose or a swift push off the bed will work if performed enough times and firmly enough. Cats are smart. They will eventually get the message. For the most persistent cases, a plant sprayer or water pistol will also get the message across.

Some cats wake their owners up in the middle of the night because they want to eat. Leaving food in the feeding bowl does not work in all cases. Some stubborn cats want their owner nearby while they eat. They get both food and attention in this way. A way of remedying this problem is to bring a bowl of food into your bedroom and allow the cat to enjoy a midnight snack while you sleep.

One cat complained loudly during the night near his food bowl, seemingly hungry despite being given a single large meal just before bedtime. To cure this disturbing habit, a remote-controlled hair dryer was set up near the feeding dish so that it went off whenever the cat meowed. He soon stopped begging for food at three in the morning.

Another method for changing a cat's nocturnal meowing behavior is to respond immediately by putting her in another room without any food or water in it. After a while, she will learn that she can snuggle next to you only if she sleeps and keeps quiet. Before you try this method, you have to be sure that your cat is not waking you up because of hunger. For cats that cry at night, leave some food and water that is easily accessible in the bedroom. It is best to feed these cats their last meal early in the evening, because cats get renewed energy after eating. Play with your cat before going to sleep so that you use up her excess energy. Tire her out, if at all possible. If nothing else works for an overactive cat, get another cat to keep her company, so that the two can wear each other out.

Another method of dealing with cats that wake you at night is the toughest of all: ignoring them. Your cat may try every trick in her repertoire to wake you, but you must disregard all of her overtures. Eventually, she will get bored and stop annoying you.

If nothing else works, you can confine her to her own nighttime lighted playroom where she has plenty of toys and other activities to keep her busy. Leaving a muted TV set playing might help distract her enough to allow you a peaceful sleep.

Cats that sleep with their people often sleep at their feet or tucked in the crook of the elbow, but some will lie on their owner's head, preferably a woman's head with lots of hair. These cats are fascinated by their owner's hair to the extent that they will chew or lick the hair while their owner is trying to sleep. Some women have resorted to wearing scarves or towels to cover up their enticing hair.

Wool Chewing

Some determined wool chewers swallow so much fabric that they develop chronic intestinal problems. Although much research has been done on this subject, the cause and cure are still baffling. Many cats, but especially the Oriental breeds such as Siamese and Burmese, are prone to this behavior. It is extremely rare in nonpedigreed cats. However, almost any cat can develop this strange appetite. Most kittens will outgrow this habit by one or two years of age. It is the persistent wool chewers that are the problem.

There are many theories as to why cats chew and eat wool, the most widely held beliefs being that the behavior is an inherited trait in some breeds, that it is a dietary deficiency causing a craving for more fiber in the diet, or that stress might be a factor. There are also those experts who believe that this ingrained habit is caused by the cat's desire for the lanolin in the wool.

Cats are also attracted to the scent of human skin, which is strong under the arms and on the feet. This explains the desire of cats to chew on your socks, with or without your feet in them. These cats also try to suck and chew the armpit region of a wool sweater because the area has a strong odor associated with sweat glands.

The addition of more fiber to the diet, such as that contained in dry food as opposed to moist food, and the addition of bones and other fibrous supplementation are

One cat with the habit of excessive sucking won't go to sleep until he sucks on both of his front paws.

beneficial in preventing the wool-chewing problem in cats. Fruits, vegetables, and grasses are also helpful because they contain plenty of fiber.

It is, of course, advisable to remove as many wool products from the reach of the cat as possible. Spraying wool products with a cheap perfume will usually keep a cat away, because cats hate the aroma of perfume. For the stubborn cat, spraying water in her face or using putrid-smelling cat repellents may help keep the wool chewing to a minimum.

Excessive Sucking

Some kittens that are deprived of a normal suckling period resort to excessive sucking on littermates, themselves, or even on their owner's skin if it is allowed. Kittens that are undernourished because of an inadequate supply of mother's milk, early weaning, or being orphaned at an early age, may resort to sucking on other objects such as stuffed toys, clothing, or other animals. They will suck on parts of the body such as ears, tails, vulvas, and scrotums of their littermates and continue doing so in adult life if allowed.

Some cats will suck on their owner's fingers or toes as if they were nursing on their mother. It is a cat's way of reducing tension and relieving stress. This behavior is most often seen during periods of relaxation. Most of the time, kneading and purring accompany the sucking. Some cats overdo this behavior to the point of causing irritation and soreness to the skin. These cats have to be disciplined whenever they attempt to lick or suck on their owner.

Cats have favorite places where they concentrate their sucking impulses. Although some suckle their toys or blankets, there are those who suck on their own tails, flanks, nipples, or paw pads. In fact, one such cat won't go to sleep until he sucks on both front paws.

This excessive sucking habit is usually infantile in nature. I have seen grown cats, larger than their mothers, nursing on her nipples, with the queen lying there allowing her "baby" to pacify himself.

When a cat licks you, it doesn't mean that she likes the salty taste of your skin. Rather, licking is a behavior that felines exhibit when they have a close attachment to a member of the family; a sort of maternal or paternal love.

If you wish to intervene and stop this habit, flick the cat gently on the nose while saying "no" firmly. Divert her attention by cuddling or playing with her.

For treating these cats, there are nasty-tasting commercial liquids available in pet stores such as Bitter Apple, or you can use strong-tasting condiments such as hot pepper sauce that will keep the cat's tongue off any object once she tastes it. She will forever remember the odor and stay away from the object. Certain body deodorant sprays or citronella sprays can be used on a person's skin to discourage the cat's sucking. Hormones may also be prescribed to help stop excessive sucking.

Excessive Vocalization

Excessive meowing can present serious problems in a cat, male or female. The meowing is often loud, high-pitched, and annoying. Usually, excessive vocalization decreases in a tomcat after neutering, but 10 to 15 percent of altered males continue to

Never reward constant meowing with attention, or the cat will persist in her irritating noisemaking.

act like intact toms even after surgery. Vocalization can be a response to pain, hunger, aggression, or a desire to hunt or roam while confined.

However, some excessive vocalization is attention-seeking. It can be a learned behavior because a cat knows that if she meows she will be picked up and probably given food to quiet her down. A case in point is a cat who was perfectly quiet all day long when he was at home alone, but whenever his mistress returned from work, he constantly vocalized until she picked him up and petted him. This was all right during the evening, but this cat meowed into the wee hours of the morning so that his mistress could not sleep. He just wanted her undivided attention. A treatment that worked in this case was to spray the cat's face with water during the night whenever he meowed excessively. His mistress was instructed to pick him up only if he was quiet. Eventually, the cat learned the difference between night and day meowing and was cured.

In the treatment of excessive meowing, it is important not to reward the cat by paying attention to her when she makes this persistent noise. Only pay attention to her and pick her up when she is quiet. Keep the cat completely confined in a room by herself so that the meowing will not be rewarded. You may also use tranquilizers prescribed by your veterinarian. These drugs are gradually reduced over a long period of time when there is a cessation of the irritating noise. More playtime with the cat will help reduce her anxiety, especially before bedtime if her vocalization is a nighttime activity. Also, give the cat lots of toys that can help keep her busy and divert her attention from herself.

Excessive Grooming

A nervous cat will tend to lick herself to the point where her fur falls out and skin lesions develop. This is seen in all cats, but mostly in Siamese and Abyssinians. Some highly nervous cats develop a neurotic compulsion that can lead to self-mutilation.

Loneliness, trauma, and jealousy may cause excessive grooming, but there may also be a physical cause. A veterinarian can rule this out.

Excessive grooming may be caused by loneliness and desire for human contact or by a tense situation. In an extremely emotional animal, there may be hair loss or itchy skin due to a traumatic occurrence in her life, such as the arrival of a new baby or a stranger in the house. Jealousy is a very strong emotion in a cat.

Some nervous queens can groom their kittens excessively to the point of mutilation. Excessive scratching and tail chasing is also seen in some nervous cats. You must try to find the cause of the stress in order to cure the animal. Hormones and tranquilizers will assist you in the treatment but will not completely cure the problem. Sometimes, all the animal needs is a little more attention, combined with more playtime and a show of love.

Tail-Biting

Although cats are relatively independent creatures, they do want attention and affection. Many nervous and high-strung cats will bite and chew on their tails for emotional reasons: loneliness, boredom, or frustration—very similar to a person's chewing on his fingernails. Also, if there is anything wrong with a cat's tail, such as an infection, the cat will often turn on the tail and attack it as if were not part of herself. What was a minor abrasion may turn into a festering and bleeding sore. If the fundamental disorder is cured, the tail-biting will probably stop.

This tail-biting habit is especially seen in kittens and could be related to the sucking instinct, but if the habit is not broken, it can persist into adulthood. For the sake of the cat's health as well as her appearance, you should discourage the habit. Sometimes tranquilizers help, and sometimes bitter-tasting preparations such as ipecac, pepper, or anti-thumbsucking medicines are used on the tail. Extract of orange and Bitter Apple are also very distasteful to most cats.

In recent years, a brain malfunction has been found that causes a cat to attack her own tail, often injuring herself severely during bouts of rage. Any breed of cat can be affected by this brain disorder, but it is seen more frequently in Siamese, Burmese, Himalayan, and Abyssinian cats. It is believed that stress can precipitate these attacks. Some cats affected by this brain malfunction can also have convulsions or will attack anything in their path, animal or human. Hormones and sedatives are helpful in controlling this disorder, but they are needed for the rest of the animal's life.

Plant-Eating

Plant-eating is a misbehavior seen in indoor cats that are never allowed outdoors where they would have access to greenery. To combat this problem, provide plenty of fresh grass and other vegetation such as oats, wheat, or catnip that you can grow in your home. This measure will usually satisfy the cat's desire for greenery and save the foliage of decorative houseplants. Chewing on houseplants is more than just feline mischief. Cats instinctively eat grass to satisfy their need for dietary fiber. Adding raw or cooked vegetables to a cat's diet may reduce their craving for your houseplants.

For plant-eating addicts, setting upside-down mousetraps under a single layer of newspaper around the plant is a wonderful deterrent. When the cat is scared (but not

Chewing on houseplants is more than just feline mischief. Cats instinctively eat grass to satisfy their need for dietary fiber.

hurt) by the spring of the mousetrap, she will eventually get the point and avoid the plant. Another method is to sprinkle hot pepper sauce or ground ginger on the houseplants, substances that are very distasteful to a cat. Try to keep the plants where the cat can't reach, such as in hanging pots. If this is not possible, spraying plants with foul-tasting and foul-smelling substances, such as a vinegar solution or Bitter Apple, will usually discourage the cat.

If you should catch your cat in the act, shout "no" and throw something at her like a ping-pong ball or a dried pea—something that won't hurt but will frighten her.

For the annoying cat that likes to dig dirt from potted plants, place cotton balls saturated with a cheap perfume or cologne around the base of the plant. Cats detest the smell of perfume and will stay away.

Moving Furniture

Some cats will knock over furniture after being disciplined too roughly or too often. Others will deliberately move objects in the house to gain attention from their owner. There is no real cure for this misbehavior, so don't provoke your cat to anger or give him any extra attention when he misbehaves. Just provide lots of regular TLC.

Masturbation

Masturbation occurs mainly in young toms that are approaching adolescence. They may mount blankets, pillows, furniture, or people's arms or legs and seemingly receive pleasure from this antic. This period of sexual excitement in a tom is usually initiated after playing with his owner. The stroking and cuddling that go along with playtime seem to excite the cat into a sexual response. If the habit is persistent or annoying to the owner, neutering will usually eliminate the problem. However, 10 to 15 percent of tomcats retain some of their masculine misbehaviors after neutering.

Occasionally, a neutered tom will masturbate, but the practice is usually not as sustained and problematic as in a natural tom. However, there are cases where a neutered tom focuses his sexual attentions on either a dog or other animal in the household. If none of these are available, he will resort to mounting toy animals or pillows for his gratification, eventually urinating on them since he can't achieve an orgasm. If this habit becomes excessive and annoying, behavior modification procedures are indicated. A squirt in the face with water is a very good deterrent to mounting a person's leg. Hormones are also very helpful in eradicating this misbehavior.

Pica (Eating Inedible Objects)

Pica is a condition in which the cat has a craving for unnatural food substitutes such as sticks, stones, wool, dirt, towels, strings, clothing, plastic bags, rubber bands, soap, and any other unlikely tidbit that appeals. It is not unusual for an extremely nervous or high-strung cat to display strange appetites. Although it is more common in dogs, some cats will eat feces, an act that may be precipitated by a biochemical disturbance in the cat's body. The behavior may also have a psychological basis.

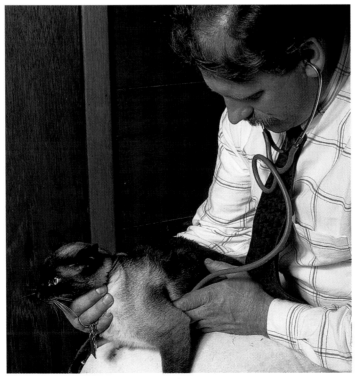

If your cat is showing a preference for inedible objects, have her tested for leukemia. See a veterinarian promptly if the cat eats anything that might be dangerous.

Abnormal Cats

Some cats indulge in pica when they are kittens, but they will usually grow out of it as they get older. The exact cause is uncertain. This odd craving could be due to a dietary deficiency, or it may be just a bad habit. It can also be a neurotic response to excessive tension in the cat's environment or to the owner's personal tension. Sometimes the condition is caused by too much attention, but more likely by too little. Boredom or insufficient exercise are also causes. A lonely or neglected cat is inclined to relieve her tensions by chewing anything available, edible or not. In these cases, obtaining a companion cat would help to relieve the boredom, as would plenty of toys (with or without catnip) for the cat to chew.

Although pica occurs in all breeds of cat, it is most commonly seen in domestic shorthairs, Siamese, Burmese, and related breeds. Some cats suffering from leukemia tend to chew, lick, and swallow various materials, from plastic and plaster to foam cups and straw mats. If your cat is showing a preference for inedible objects, it is advisable to have her tested for leukemia.

I have a regular feline patient named Rufus. He eats anything that doesn't eat him first. He considers brooms, brushes, cardboard boxes, and especially plastic objects to be gourmet delicacies. I have had to perform abdominal surgery twice to relieve immovable blockages in his intestinal tract. He'll never learn. No amount of psychological counseling seems to be helping this not-so-picky eater.

If your cat is eating unsuitable objects, find a proper substitute for her to chew on, such as intriguing toys made of a variety of materials, including rubber, cloth, or plastic—possibly laced with catnip to get her attention.

For nervous and high-strung cats, it is sometimes advisable to give mood-elevating and antidepressant drugs to suppress the desire to eat unnatural things.

To help stop occurrences of pica, it is wise to make sure your cat is provided with a completely balanced diet and supplementary vitamins and minerals. Divert your cat from temptation by moving all possible undesirable chewable objects out of reach. If this is not possible, you can spray the items that you want to protect with all types of bitter-tasting and foul-smelling substances.

Jumping on Counters

Cats will usually jump on tables or counters only when the owners are not around, because they know that if they are caught they'll be disciplined.

One smart Siamese, Ming, has a deal worked out with the dog in the house. Ming knocks food off the counter, and the dog joins in to help enjoy the repast.

To help thwart a jumping cat, booby-trap the counters with upside-down mousetraps that will startle but not hurt the cat. Cover the mousetrap with newspaper so the cat can't see the trap. Eventually you will be able to eliminate the mousetrap, because the cat will be afraid to walk on the paper for fear of setting the trap off. Alternatively, place plastic or tin plates on the edge of the counter, half on and half off. When the cat jumps on the counter, she will invariably knock the pan off, causing it to fall with a loud bang. Some owners have used electronic gadgets to scare their misbehaving cats, such as the shock mats that are designed to scare cats off furniture or counters. The mats give off a mild, stimulating shock to punish the cats for unwanted behavior.

For cats that love to tear up paper, an empty grocery bag is sheer joy. Don't tempt these cats by leaving important papers lying around.

It might take several weeks, but these methods will help the cat learn which objects are off-limits.

Paper Fetish

Dennis is a paper freak that will attack any type of paper product within his reach. He chews, shreds, and destroys paper with a vengeance, and he seems to enjoy the crinkling and ripping sound as he tears it into little pieces. Once the paper is in shreds, the cat walks away perfectly content, without eating any of it. Tearing up paper is a difficult habit to overcome, so it is best not to tempt a cat by leaving valuable papers lying around.

You can provide a cat like Dennis with empty grocery bags, corrugated boxes, and other cardboard products that are more durable than flimsy paper ones. There are also toys that are made of material that sounds like paper crinkling.

If you have any valuable objects made of paper, you can protect them by repelling the offending feline. You can use sticky paper, malodorous solutions smeared on the paper, upside-down mousetraps under the paper, and electronic burglar alarms to scare the culprit.

Diet-Related Misbehaviors

As is the case with other behaviors, the eating habits of cats are subject to change under stress. The cat's most common response to stress is to stop eating. A period of suppressed appetite lasting one or two days is rather typical in a normally healthy, well-nourished cat following the introduction of a newcomer to the home, a stint of boarding, or a family's move to a new house. Under such circumstances, the owner should be prepared to offset any negative reactions in the cat by providing her with the kind of loving attention that can be so easily diverted elsewhere at the birth of a baby or during the upheaval of changing households.

A cat that has not eaten for an extended period should never be ignored. Anorexia nervosa, a refusal of food over long periods of time with no observable physical cause, has been experimentally induced in cats by placing them in extremely distressing situations. Cats have been known to starve to death this way. Dangerously suppressed appetites can develop in the home environment, and without professional intervention, a pet may die.

A less common neurotic response to stress is overeating. Indiscriminate and voracious eating of a compulsive nature has nothing to with normal bodily needs. It is a phenomenon not dissimilar to compulsive overeating in humans. Again, professional intervention is indicated.

The type of food, the quality and quantity, and the feeding schedule can often cause behavior problems in cats. The feline temperament causes a cat to resist any quick change, whether it be in the diet or when strangers show up in the household.

Most cats hate disruptions in their lifestyle. Once a cat is set in her habits, any deviation from the routine may cause behavior problems such as spraying or aggression toward the owner or other pets in the household.

A sudden change of diet may cause the cat to go on a hunger strike. More devious cats may begin house-soiling, spraying, or committing aggressive acts. A good rule to follow with any cat is to show patience and deliberation in making any changes.

The time of feeding and the brand of cat food may be very important to the cat. Some cats only want dry food, while others will only eat table scraps. It is best to treat each cat as an individual.

Female cats may become finicky due to their periodic hormonal changes. They might show a change in their eating habits during their heat cycle, pregnancy, or nursing phases. If a queen loses a great deal of weight during these phases, it is best to spay her and eliminate these hormonal problems.

Finicky Eaters

I'm sure you don't have enough fingers to count the number of times you have discovered a food that your cat has found irresistible, at least for a couple of meals. You probably stocked up on this latest favorite, only to be looked at with disdain when you attempted to serve this food again. Quite often you have probably gotten the same scornful look when the food dish contained a really old favorite.

None of this is necessarily honest-to-goodness finickiness, because so many factors affect the appetite of the cat. At the top of the list is odor. The sense of smell is so acute in the cat that a repugnant odor or the inability to smell could actually cause the animal to starve to death. For example, I know of one colony of cats that stopped eating because the detergent used to clean their food dishes had been changed. Also, any infection in the upper respiratory tract will prevent a cat from eating, simply because she cannot smell the food.

Is your cat a finicky eater? Some cats get bored with the same food day in and day out.

Abnormal Cats

Because healthy cats can go without food for very long periods, they can steadfastly refuse food they dislike almost to the point of starvation. Many cats do get bored with the same food day in and day out.

The immediate surroundings at mealtime can also ruin a cat's appetite. More light and more noise than usual, as well as extra people around, will send most cats scurrying for a quiet, secluded spot. Even raised voices of the master and mistress or other members of the family cannot be tolerated by most cats. Everything has to be just right, especially for the shy and timid cat.

The temperature of the food can also be a factor. Most cats do not like cold food, so it should not be served directly from the refrigerator. Brought to room temperature or mixed with a little warm water, food will be much more palatable.

Uneaten food that has become soggy and contaminated should be thrown out. It is unacceptable to any self-respecting cat. In addition, any food that is unfit for human consumption should *never* be offered to a cat.

Some eccentric cats like to eat tuna and nothing else. They will go on a hunger strike if they don't get their tuna. However, this diet will cause a nutritional deficiency necessitating medication. For these cats, you should mix regular cat food in with the tuna, gradually increasing the amount of cat food so the cat receives nutrients other than those found in tuna.

Overeaters

Although most cats are fastidious eaters, there are some that are indiscriminate, devouring any type of food they encounter. Some cats will eat vegetables, olives, corn-on-the-cob, pickles, and other varieties of food not in a cat's normal diet. For liquid refreshment, some cats are full of surprises, drinking anything from tea and orange juice to beer.

Food Allergies that Affect Behavior

The veterinary profession has established that certain foods cause all types of strange reactions in cats, including behavior problems.

In one case, a certain brand of canned food caused severe itching in a cat, causing her to engage in frenzied grooming. Constant open lesions on her skin were treated, and all types of tranquilizers and sedatives were administered to stop the severe licking and biting, but to no avail. Finally the specific brand of canned food was eliminated from the cat's diet, and the excessive grooming soon ceased. The "incurable" skin lesions rapidly healed. This case illustrates how important it is to consider changing a cat's diet in connection with any chronic misbehavior problem.

Water Bowl Eccentricity

There are some cranky cats that do not want to drink water that is near their food dish. It is believed that these cats are reverting to their instincts from the wild, where they did not eat and drink in the same location. Other eccentric cats will drink water only from dripping faucets, toilet bowls, soap dishes, and other odd places. Experts believe

Many cranky cats will find fault with the size, cleanliness, or placement of their water dish. Because drinking water is so important, it may be necessary to cater to the whims of your pet on this issue.

Jealousy and competition in a multiple-cat household can cause problems at mealtime. Feeding each cat on his or her own dish may help.

they do this because cats dislike getting their whiskers wet while lapping water in a small bowl. Be sure to use large water bowls to suit the whims of your pet.

Diet as a Cause of Spraying

It is important to consider diet and type of food as a possible cause of spraying. A case in point concerns an adult, well-behaved cat that was suddenly put on a prescription diet for an intestinal condition. The cat rejected the new food, even to the point of spraying in his food dish. He was trying to tell the owner of his displeasure with the new food. The treatment was fairly simple—a gradual resumption of the original food, with a few minor changes so as not to aggravate his intestinal problem.

Another cause of diet-related spraying is jealousy, which is a strong emotion in a cat. The jealousy can be caused by another cat, animal, or person. It can also be caused by envy of a different diet that looks and smells better than what a cat is usually served. A case that illustrates this situation is that of a well-behaved, neutered cat that began spraying when the diet of the other cat in the household was changed to a more palatable, prescription diet because of a medical condition. The misbehaving cat concentrated his spraying in the cats' feeding area, usually spraying in the dish of the other cat. After consultation with the veterinarian, the diet of the culprit was changed to the same prescription diet that smelled so good. He was content with this arrangement, and the spraying ceased.

Hunger

Hunger in a cat can cause all types of behavioral problems, such as excessive meowing, spraying, and house-soiling. Some cats become anxious and fretful when they are hungry. Each cat is an individual when it comes to the amount of food that they require for contentment. Some cats, just like some humans, have a greater metabolic need and require more food than others.

Excessive meowing should be a signal to the owner that something is wrong. It means that the cat is upset about something, whether it be the environment or just plain hunger. It could be her way of begging for more food. She doesn't sit up and beg like a dog might but just makes a lot of noise to attract your attention. If the meowing doesn't stop after an offer of more food, look for other causes.

Vomiting

Vomiting can sometimes be caused by environmental factors. There are some cats that will eat voraciously—more than their stomachs can hold—because of a strange cat in the vicinity. A cat that feels insecure will overeat before the other cat can get at her food. It would be wise to feed a cat like this in a private, quiet place—somewhere the cat feels secure. It may also help to feed her small amounts at a time, so that she doesn't gorge herself. A high-strung, nervous cat is more apt to vomit than a sedate cat.

There are behavior changes that can occur as a result of feeding certain types of food. I have had patients who are allergic to a specific canned or dry food and vomit because of it.

Unlike single cats that are prone to boredom and overeating, cats in multi-cat households tend to be more active. All cats need regular exercise.

Abnormal Cats

Single-Cat Syndrome

Cats that are lonely and bored do the same things that people do—sit around all day and eat whenever food or snacks are available. Vets have been seeing more obesity in cats in recent years. In a single-cat household, most cats are getting fatter because they do not move around much, especially if they are completely indoor cats. They lie around watching people or TV, whichever is nearby. These cats need some sort of aerobic activity or playtime with their owners to get exercise, which is imperative for good health.

In a multi-cat household, the hostility within the group usually keeps the cats more active, vying for food and affection from people. These cats usually get enough exercise playing with one another.

Food Games

There are cats that combine eating with playful antics, some of which can be annoying to their owners. Young cats in particular like to scatter dry food all over the floor and then chase and pounce on it as if it were prey. After chasing each piece of food for a while, a cat eventually works up an appetite and will go around the floor, eating one tiny piece of food at a time. To counteract this messy habit, entice the feline to play with ping-pong balls and other toys that will divert her attention.

One cat I know has a bizarre way of eating his food. When he dines, he takes a few bites of his food, then puts his foot in the bowl and moves the bowl a short distance away. However, before he puts his foot in the bowl to move it again, he licks all the food off his paw from the previous move. He repeats this odd behavior until all the food is gone and he has traveled all over the kitchen. Another eccentric feline will only eat from a bowl if it is filled to the top. If it is half empty, he will not deign to eat.

When cats are hungry, they use body language. They head-butt and writhe around your legs. Cats are smart. They know they can get rewards for these antics.

Therapy for Dietary Misbehaviors

A nervous cat is more apt to suffer a loss of appetite than a placid cat with a quiet disposition. Any annoying incident around the house can affect her appetite. One of the best treatments for a cat that is upset about something is to put her in a dark and quiet place with her food and water. She will feel more secure away from the stressful situation.

PROBLEMS OF MULTI-CAT FAMILIES

In multi-cat households, you are likely to encounter more behavior problems than with a single pet, because the animals revert to the basic instincts of their species. You may see aggression, scent-marking, and house destruction. The more cats you have, the more dilemmas you will face.

As with any group of people, you will also find many different types of personalities within the cat household. There may be many battles before a dominant cat takes over. Furthermore, the losers may take out their frustrations with inappropriate behavior, including house-soiling, spraying, or destroying rugs, furniture, curtains, or other expensive objects.

Mealtime is a very critical time in a multi-cat household. A cat should know that she has a certain locale for her food dish. Feed cats in separate rooms if necessary, because some cats become aggressive at mealtime. Some bullies will chase away the more timid cats, so try to supervise their activity during this period.

Stress

Problems can arise that cause much stress in a multi-cat family. Most of the time, the majority of cats will develop close and friendly relationships, but sometimes there will be a constant source of irritation between or among two or more cats. Both cats, the pursuer and the one being pursued, will show signs of anxiety and stress. The bully will cause the harassed cat to hide and be reluctant to move around the house, a situation affecting his eating and litter box habits. Jealousy between cats is a frequent source of trouble in a multi-cat family.

In every group of cats, some will be dominant and some will be submissive. Try to give each cat plenty of attention individually, with play and feeding periods away from the others.

In an unhappy household, where people are yelling at each other and fighting most of the time, the cats react with all kinds of misbehaviors.

Introducing a New Cat

If you are considering bringing a new cat into a multi-cat family, it is wise to introduce a kitten rather than an adult cat. There is a much better chance of harmony among cats

When introducing a new cat into a multi-cat family, confine the new cat in a single room for a few days, allowing resident cats to get used to the odors of the new pet.

if the kitten has been properly socialized by being allowed to stay with her mother and siblings a few weeks beyond weaning age. It is suggested that kittens to be brought into multi-cat households be 12 weeks of age instead of the normal weaning age of 8 weeks. Such kittens usually fare better in a household with other cats.

When introducing a new cat into a multi-cat family, confine the new cat in a single room for a few days, allowing resident cats to get used to the odors of the new pet. After a few days, let the new cat walk around the house under your supervision so the older cats can check her out. Put her back in the isolated room, and each day allow her out more and more.

Always give top priority to the resident cat or cats in terms of feeding and affection, because they will be jealous if you show too much attention to the newcomer. The resident cats will certainly be antagonistic to the newcomer. You can reduce this animosity by telling the resident animals that you still love them; they'll understand. If the family plans to have two cats, opposite sexes will be better friends, with less fighting and less tension. Experience has also shown that an even number of cats makes for more harmonious households than an odd number.

It is important to realize that too many cats in one household may be detrimental to the emotional and physical well-being of some of the more insecure ones. Overcrowding may change a peaceful cat into an aggressive and misbehaving rogue. These aggressive cats live in a tense state most of the time and do not behave normally. Be sure to give the cats plenty of space in the house where they can relax and be alone. All cats like quiet time.

Shy, Timid Cats

In multi-cat households, it will take a lot of work and patience to get the shy cat to feel comfortable around the other cats. Introduce the timid one slowly to the other cats and only at a time when the other cats are asleep or in a very relaxed state. Never try to get the cats together at feeding time, because tempers are usually at a high pitch when food is nearby. The introduction should be done gradually, so that it may sometimes take weeks and weeks of careful supervision. In severe cases of intimidation, mood-elevating drugs may have to be prescribed to calm the nerves of the fearful cat.

Some shy and timid cats may never be conditioned to live with other cats, and it would be best to put these cats in a situation where they are the only animals around. This, plus lots of tender loving care, will go a long way to assure them a normal life.

Most cats, though not all, are happier when there are multiple cats in the household, but too many cats can also upset a shy and timid cat that is pushed away both physically and emotionally. The more extroverted cats give her an inferiority complex that serves to compound her emotional instability. She hides most of the day, coming out of her hiding places when the other cats are not around. This state of affairs will affect her eating habits, because some of the other cats will bully her and deprive her of her food. There is definitely a pecking order with multiple cats in a household. The mentally and physically strong will dominate.

Reducing Stress

We all need space sometimes, and the same is true for cats. In a home with more than one cat, a cat might occasionally feel closed in and may need more quiet time by

Too many cats in the house can upset a shy and timid cat. Shy cats may hide most of the day, coming out only when the other cats are not around.

151

To relieve anxiety in cats that need more personal space, install artificial perches so that they can get some peace and security. Having their own territory helps cats cope with stress.

herself. To relieve anxiety in these cases, provide the cat with places to get away from the other cats for a while. You can install artificial trees, shelves, or other objects so that a cat can sit in high places and get some peace and security.

House-Soiling

House-soiling in a multi-cat family may present a problem, as it is sometimes difficult to determine which cat is the culprit. You can isolate all the individual cats with their own litter boxes to see which one is doing the messing. If that doesn't work, your veterinarian can give you a pill to discolor the urine of a suspected cat.

If a cat is soiling in the house, it may be because one dominant cat is chasing her out of the litter box. Be sure to have enough well-placed boxes throughout the house so that a submissive cat can find one that is secluded and away from the bully. In many cases, the dominant cat is attempting to take over as the leader and will challenge the newcomer or submissive cat while she is in her toilet area.

In some cases, the reason for house-soiling has a simple solution. If too many cats are using the same litter box, eliminations will occur outside the box. There should be one litter box for each cat in the household.

An interesting and perplexing case concerns a five-cat family where inappropriate urination was quite prevalent in the household. However, the day that one of the cats, named Pepper, died, the misbehavior ceased completely. It could have been due to a personality clash Pepper had with the other cats, but it was probably due to jealousy. Pepper had been a frail and sickly cat and received much of the attention and only gourmet food, because she did not like the regular cat food. The owners carried her in their arms quite a bit, talking baby talk and words of endearment. Once Pepper was gone, the other cats' rebellion ceased.

Spraying

In a multi-cat household, there is apt to be much spraying because of the cats' territorial instincts. If there is one particular cat in the group that is doing the spraying, it is a good idea to give him time by himself while the other cats are confined to one part of the house. This time alone reassures him that he is still the number-one cat in the family. Give him lots of attention and lots of loving. Treat him as a special individual and give him his own food and litter boxes—the VIP treatment.

If a new cat is introduced into a multi-cat family and an outbreak of spraying occurs, it means that you have reached a saturation point and the other cats will not accept the newcomer. Rather than cause a lot of problems, it probably would be best to find another home for the new cat. However, a commercially available feline pheromone spray is sometimes helpful in reducing tension when several cats live together. When used persistently, it can reduce or eliminate inappropriate spraying.

All cats crave time alone with their owner. This special attention—the VIP treatment—is particularly important for misbehaving cats.

Abnormal Cats

Fighting

In every group of cats, there is a wide variety of temperaments and personalities very similar to that found in a family of humans. Some cats will coexist peacefully within a household, while others will defend their territory by fighting or spraying to show their displeasure and define their territory. Sparring between cats is fairly normal until one asserts his or her dominance over the others. If the fighting does not abate on its own, you must intervene and separate the cats in different quarters with their own food dishes and litter boxes. In severe cases, tranquilizers may help reduce the antagonism. Individual petting will help soothe a nervous cat, but remember that feline jealousy is a strong emotion. It is best to initiate petting when the other cats are out of sight, lest envy rear its ugly head.

As with people, having two or more cats in any household may provoke disputes. Sudden aggression may start for no apparent reason to us, but the cats have their own motives. Try to determine what is causing the problem—possibly it could be jealousy or simply a scent on one cat's fur that is objectionable to the other. If this seems to be so, use a damp towel to rub the cat down in order to neutralize the foreign odor.

If one cat is a bully and is intimidating the other cats, you might have to resort to tranquilizers to slow him or her down. Sometimes, a simpler solution such as placing a bell on the cat's collar will help. For a timid cat, mood elevators and hormones will help instill more courage.

It may be difficult to tell when fighting between two cats becomes excessive. Most of the time, cat fights are either play-fighting or a normal, temporary territory clash.

Occasionally, you will find two cats that simply hate each other, but most cats can learn to tolerate each other. Over time, some will even become the best of friends.

A Clash of Personalities

Occasionally, you find two neutered male or female cats that will not tolerate each other under any circumstances. No matter what therapy is tried, nothing works. These cats hate each other and will fight at the slightest provocation. Of course, this situation also occurs in the human race when two people just don't like each other.

In the case of a clash, you have to attempt to desensitize the cats to each other. Try to get them used to one another by using sight, sounds, and smells.

Confine each cat to a separate room, allowing one cat only in that room so that her scent is imparted to all the furnishings. Then trade rooms, so that each cat can get the scent of the other cat in her own room. Eventually bring both cats (in crates) to a new room, a neutral area, and place them facing each other. Leave them for a short while at first, gradually increasing the time they are looking at one another.

Eventually, allow the cats out of their crates with a barrier between them so that each can roam around her side of the room while eyeing the other cat. After a while you can lower the barrier so that they are in the room together, but only when you can supervise them. Talk to both cats, complimenting them in a soothing voice so that they can feel comfortable with each other.

As a last resort, tranquilizers and hormones may be used to aid in the acceptance process. It is important that the resident cat gets used to the odors of the new addition and sees that there is no threat to his or her domination. It might take weeks of concerted effort to accomplish this feat completely, but if some measure of peace is not reached in one month, I would advise finding the new addition another home.

About the Author

The author with one of his favorite well-trained cats, Savannah, owned by Linda Sturdy, at Zanzbar Restaurant in Fort Lauderdale, Florida.

Dr. Louis Vine, author of nearly a dozen pet books, attended Cornell and Middlesex Universities. He has been practicing veterinary medicine in Chapel Hill, North Carolina, for more than 40 years and is a frequent lecturer and demonstrator at veterinary symposiums. Professional journals carry his articles on varied subjects in veterinary medicine. Dr. Vine is a member of the American Veterinary Society of Animal Behavior and the International Animal Behavior Society.

Dr. Vine's first book, *Dogs in My Life,* published in 1961, was widely acclaimed in the United States and Great Britain and has been translated into several European languages, as have many of his subsequent books. Dr. Vine is also the author of *The Total Dog Book,* which was proclaimed "Best Technical Book of the Year" by the Dog Writers Association of America, Inc. His book *Common Sense Book of Complete Cat Care* was chosen as an alternate selection for the Literary Guild Book Club and was published in a revised edition in 1992.

For T.F.H. Publications, Dr. Vine has written *Training Problem Dogs* and *A Vet's Advice About Puppies* in addition to this book.

Index

Index

Index

R

Ragdoll, 32
Rage, 76
Rattling can, 17, 20
Reinforcement, 13, 15, 25
Remote punishment, 20
Retraining therapy, 11-13
Rewards, 11-12, 28-29
Rex, 32
Russian Blue, 32

S

Savannah, 41
Scolding, 19
Scratching instinct, 37
Scratching posts, 37, 109-112
Scratching, 25, 37
Scratching, destructive, 108
Self-image, 29
Self-mutilation, 89
Senile cat and litter box, 116
Sensitivity of cats, 31, 89-92
Separation anxiety, 94
Sexual instinct, 34
Shock mats, 18
Shoulder-riding, 58
Shyness, 70, 150-151
Siamese, 31, 32, 133, 136, 137, 140
Sick cat and litter box, 116
Single-cat syndrome, 148
Skin glands, 36
Social conflict, 87
Social isolation, 87
Socialization, 6, 31, 72, 150
Somali, 31
Spaying, effects of, 26
Spraying, 127, 146, 153
Strangers, pet's conflict with, 11, 87
Stress, causes and effects in cats, 26, 86-93, 149

Sucking, excessive, 134
Suckling instinct, 34

T

Tail-biting, 137
Tail-chasing, 89
Tail language, 39
Television, effects of, 67
Territorial aggression, 84
Territorial instinct, 36
Territorial responses, 88
Thunderstorms, fear of, 13, 101
"Time-out" method, 21-22
Timidity, 70
Toilet-training instinct, 39
Tonkinese, 32
Tranquilizers, 11, 14, 64, 72, 77, 78, 83, 92, 102, 128, 136, 154, 155

U

Unhappy cats, 60
Unpleasant experiences, 88
Urination, spiteful, 121
Urine-marking, 37, 130

V

Vacuum activity, 46
Valium, 14, 78
Veterinarian, 6-7, 8, 61, 63, 75, 79, 90, 97, 139, 140, 146
Vinegar, 108, 125, 126, 138
Vocabularies, feline, 23
Vocalization, excessive, 67, 88, 135, 147
Vomiting, 89, 105, 147

W

Water bowl eccentricity, 144
Water gun, 17, 21, 113, 132
Water phobia or fetish, 51, 102
Water spray, 17, 113
Wool chewing, 133